Troll Teacher Ideas

TestWise

Intermediate

Strategies for Success on Standardized Tests

Prepare your students in Grades 4–6 to take nationally normed standardized tests

Eleanor S. Angeles
Edward C. Haggerty

Contents

This edition published in 2002.
ISBN: 0-8167-4163-7
Printed in the United States of America
10 9 8 7 6 5 4 3 2

The Objectives of *TestWise*

TestWise: Strategies for Success on Standardized Tests is designed to help you prepare your students to take any of the three most common nationally-normed tests: the CAT, or California Achievement Test; the CTBS, or Comprehensive Test of Basic Skills; and the ITBS, the Iowa Test of Basic Skills®.

The most effective way to prepare your students for the reading, math, and study skills content of these standardized tests is to guide your students to do their very best in what you teach them in class. Nothing can replace the day-to-day growth in competence that good teaching fosters. The purpose of *TestWise* is to help you familiarize your students with the formats that standardized tests use and to help them master basic test-taking strategies that will improve their scores and make them more confident and self-assured when they sit down to take the actual test.

To use the strategies and tests in *TestWise* with your students, reproduce the appropriate pages in this book. For added convenience, you may wish to purchase sufficient quantities of *TestWise* to use as a classroom set.

How *TestWise Intermediate* is Organized

TestWise Intermediate is divided into eight tests. These tests correspond to the eight skill areas tested on the CAT, the CTBS, and the ITBS. In turn, each of the eight main test sections in *TestWise Intermediate* is divided into three parts:

1. **Learn About the Strategies**—a one-page introduction to the testing strategies most appropriate for the content of the particular test. The Coach's Corner feature explains the chosen strategies for each test and reinforces the most beneficial strategies throughout the tests.

2. **Practice the Strategies**—One or more short subtests that let students put the strategies into practice. Special self-directed comments on these pages help make the strategies real. They

   - model when to use a particular strategy

     > What are the directions telling me to do?

   - explain how to apply a strategy to a particular testing situation

     > I'll tell myself what the underlined words mean. Then I'll check the answers.

   - offer positive self-encouragement

     > I know I can put every answer in the correct spot on the answer sheet if I pay attention.

3. **Timed Practice Test/Use the Strategies on Your Own**—students can take a multipart vocabulary, reading comprehension, or other content area test in circumstances that come closer to what they will experience when they take the actual test. You may choose to time the tests or not, as best fits your students' needs. If you time the tests, use the times suggested in the chart that follows.

Suggested Times for the Timed Practice Tests

1. Vocabulary	*30 min.*		**5.** Language Expression	*40 min.*
2. Reading Comprehension	*40 min.*		**6.** Mathematical Computation	*30 min.*
3. Spelling	*20 min.*		**7.** Mathematical Concepts and Applications	*50 min.*
4. Language Mechanics	*15 min.*		**8.** Reference and Study Skills	*30 min.*

Using the Pages

Answers

The answers for the questions on a page are given below each answer grid. Before you duplicate a page with an answer grid, you might want to make a single copy first and either cut off the answers or draw a line through them with a marker to make them unreadable. If you wish, you may leave the answers on the page and have students correct their own pages. For your convenience, if you use the answer sheet for the Timed Practice Tests, answer keys are reprinted at the back of this book.

In the perfect world, the students master all the strategies and get all the answers right. Since everything is rarely perfect, it's more important that students develop the thinking habits that the strategies encourage. When you use *TestWise*, therefore, you empower your students to do well on the actual test if you stress the strategies rather than the answers.

The *Practice the Strategies* Pages

Orally go over the sample item at the start of each subtest. Point out the answer grid at the bottom of the page. Have them mark in the answer to the sample question and then complete the rest of the subtest on their own.

After students finish the Practice the Strategies test, go over the answers. Invite students to explain how they reached each correct answer. Use the chalkboard or chart paper to record useful strategies your students themselves devise.

The Timed Practice Tests

Students should do each end-of-section Timed Practice Test on their own in class. If your students need a quick review of content to build their confidence, you might want to go over the sample questions at the start of each Practice the Strategies subtest in that section of *TestWise*.

After each Timed Practice Test, go over the answers with your students. Then ask students to discuss how they used the strategies to help them choose their answers.

When to Start

There are thirty short Practice the Strategies tests and eight longer Timed Practice Tests. We recommend starting to use *TestWise* forty to sixty class days before your class is scheduled to take the standardized test your school or school district uses. Keep your *TestWise* work positive and low key. You don't want to inadvertently foster test anxiety in your students.

A Closer Look at the Standardized Tests

The nationally normed standardized test is a familiar feature of the American educational landscape. No matter whether you support the tests' validity, decry their obtrusiveness, or take the middle ground between these two positions, you want your students to do well on the tests. Your students' success reflects your school's success. Good scores please parents, politicians, and the community at large.

One problem is that students take the CAT, the CTBS, or the ITBS at most only once a year and, in many school districts, less frequently. If you drove your car only once a year, how effective would your driving skills be? If you had to take a road test once a year but never even sat in a car at any other time, how prepared would you feel? In many ways, the annual testing ritual forces young test-takers to face similar obstacles. What can you do to help them perform their best?

Help Your Students Work Smart...

When they prepare for taking the test
Make sure that your students become comfortable and well practiced in applying the proven test-taking strategies in *TestWise*.

Build mastery of test-taking strategies the way you handle reading strategies. Discuss them, remind students to use them, and reinforce how they're used. After a practice test, discuss not just the answers but also the strategies the students used to find them. These follow-up discussions encourage peer coaching, as students learn from one another what strategies they used and how best to implement them. Be open to additional strategies that the students suggest (as long as you believe the strategies will work).

When they complete name grids and answer grids
Name grids and answer grids are necessary for machine-scoring the tests and reporting the results accurately. But carelessness, anxiety, inattention to detail, and other personal factors cause students to make avoidable mistakes on these forms. Students often darken the wrong circles under their names, put their names or part of their names in the wrong place, and substitute the current year for the year of their birth.

To sidestep mistakes, some teachers fill in the name grids for their classes before they distribute the test booklets. You can also get students accustomed to completing these grids correctly by doing dry runs beforehand and making the activity into a game. Have students develop personal strategies for keeping their place and for putting in the right information. On testing day students will be familiar with these grids and less likely to make careless mistakes. You will find copies of a name grid, directions, and answer sheet on pages 8–10 of *TestWise*.

All the tests in *TestWise* have answer grids at the bottom of each page. For practice using separate answer sheets, duplicate the answer sheet on page 9 and have students use it when they take the Timed Practice Tests in *TestWise*.

When they interpret directions
One of the key contributors to success on standardized tests is the ability to understand and follow activity directions. Following directions is a skill you can build and reinforce throughout the year. The strategies reminders in *TestWise* will continually tell students to rephrase test directions in their own words and take responsibility for knowing what they are asked to do. You can apply this strategy to all written and oral activity directions you give your students throughout the year.

When they encounter different formats

TestWise gives practice in using all the formats that students will encounter on the ITBS, the CAT, and the CTBS. In most cases the answer choices are printed in a single column and are labeled by a letter in dark type next to each choice. Help students notice that the letters F–G–H–J (or J–K–L–M, depending on the test) alternate with A–B–C–D to identify the choices. Point out how the pattern helps them mark the correct choice in the answer grid. If they go to darken in Ⓐ and find Ⓕ instead, they know they are putting the answer in the wrong place. It's a clue to check the question number.

As an exercise, have students discuss the question numbers on a typical test page in *TestWise*. Students should notice that item numbers run down a page, not across. Encourage students who have difficulty keeping their place to devise a personal strategy for knowing the item number of the question they are working on. Some students always keep a finger pointed at the item number.

Occasionally students will encounter a multiple-choice format that labels the choices in a different way. For example, in the following sample item from Language Mechanics, the test-taker needs to pick which part of the sentence contains a mistake in capitalization.

On thursday	the whole school visited	the Milton Museum of Art.	
A	**B**	**C**	**D** None

Encourage students to notice how answer choices are presented.

When they don't know an answer and want to guess

The Iowa Test of Basic Skills penalizes students for guessing. The CAT and CTBS do not. Therefore, depending on the test your students are taking, tell them whether they should guess at an answer or leave a test item blank.

The best strategy for guessing is to eliminate first as many wrong answer choices as possible and then pick the remaining choice that seems more likely to be correct. If none of the answer choices seem incorrect, students taking the ITBS will do better not to guess.

If students leave items on the answer sheet blank, caution them to take extra care when they darken in the circle for the next answer. They must be sure that the item number and the answer number are the same. Otherwise, all following answers will be in the wrong circles and thus incorrect.

When they experience test anxiety

First, try to forestall test anxiety if you can. Reassure the nervous that they already know how to do everything that's on the test. They don't have to be perfect; they just have to answer the questions they know. Tell them that they'll be learning all sorts of good strategies to help them do well, and express your confidence in them and their abilities. Don't let your work in *TestWise* be a cause of test anxiety. Be supportive. Help kids stretch. Keep the tone light and don't use the threat of failure on the test as a bludgeon to make students work harder. Reluctance to take practice tests may be due to fear and uncertainty. Do what you must to encourage each student do his or her best. Learning to take deep breaths also helps students relax.

When tomorrow is testing day

To do their best, students should be well rested and ready to work. Write a note to families encouraging them to make sure their children get a good night's sleep before the test. Families should also make sure that children have a nourishing breakfast on testing day.

Getting Started: The Name Grid and Answer Sheet

To the Teacher
Read these directions aloud. Have the class work with you to fill out a name grid.

A successful start will set a positive tone for the rest of the test. Make sure your students don't get rattled by the name grid, as many do.

Before your students take the actual test, practice completing a name grid.

Strategies
Remind students to use the following strategies:
- Listen carefully
- Put the directions in your own words. Tell yourself what the directions want you to do.
- Use your fingers to keep your place.

Afterwards, have students discuss which strategies worked best for them. Then, as a follow-up, practice completing another name grid in a day or two.

The Answer Sheet
You may choose to have students record their answers to the Timed Practice Tests on the answer sheet on pages 9 and 10 instead of in the answer space at the bottom of each test page.

1. Find the words *Last Name* and *First Name*.

- Print your last name in the boxes under the words *last name*. Write one letter in each box. Print your first name in the boxes directly under the words *first name*. If there are not enough spaces for your full name, print as many letters as you can. If your name has a hyphen or an apostrophe, leave it out.

- Now put a finger on the letter you wrote in the first box. Use that finger to go down the column to find the circled letter that matches the letter you wrote in the box. Now darken the circled letter. Do this for each letter in your name. Be sure you darken only one letter in each column.

2. Darken the correct circle for *Male* or *Female*.

3. Write the number of your grade in the box labeled *Grade*. For example, if you are in the fourth grade, write the number 4.

4. Find the words *Birth Date* and the words *month*, *day*, and *year*.

- Below the word *month* write the name of the month in which you were born. If you were born in May, you would write *May*. Then in the column below, you would darken the circle next to *May*. Now it's your turn. Write the name of the month in which you were born. Darken the circle next to the name of the month.

- Under the word *day* write the number of the day on which you were born. Use a two-number date. If you were born on May 27, you would write the numbers *2* and *7*. If you were born on May 1, you would write the numbers *0* and *1*. Now it's your turn. Write the two numbers that give the date on which you were born. Now below the date you wrote, darken one number in the first column and one number in the second column.

- Under the word *year*, in the space after the number *19*, write the last two numbers of the year in which you were born. Do not write the numbers for *this year*. You were not born this year. If you were born in 1989, you would write *89* in the box. Then you would darken the *8* in the first column and the *9* in the second column. Now it's your turn. Write the last two numbers of the year in which you were born. Now below the number of the year you wrote, darken one number in the first column and one number in the second column.

| Last Name | First Name | | Male O Female O | Grade |

Birth Date

MONTH	DAY	YEAR
		19
JAN O	(0) (0)	(1) (1)
FEB O	(1) (1)	(2) (2)
MAR O	(2) (2)	(3) (3)
APR O	(3) (3)	(4) (4)
MAY O	(4)	(5) (5)
JUNE O	(5)	(6) (6)
JULY O	(6)	(7) (7)
AUG O	(7)	(8) (8)
SEPT O	(8)	(9) (9)
OCT O	(9)	(0) (0)
NOV O		
DEC O		

Troll

TestWise
Intermediate

Strategies for Success on
Standardized Tests

TEST 1. Vocabulary

1 (A)(B)(C)(D) 10 (F)(G)(H)(J) 19 (A)(B)(C)(D) 28 (A)(B)(C)(D) 37 (F)(G)(H)(J) 46 (A)(B)(C)(D)
2 (F)(G)(H)(J) 11 (A)(B)(C)(D) 20 (F)(G)(H)(J) 29 (F)(G)(H)(J) 38 (A)(B)(C)(D) 47 (F)(G)(H)(J)
3 (A)(B)(C)(D) 12 (F)(G)(H)(J) 21 (A)(B)(C)(D) 30 (A)(B)(C)(D) 39 (F)(G)(H)(J) 48 (A)(B)(C)(D)
4 (F)(G)(H)(J) 13 (A)(B)(C)(D) 22 (F)(G)(H)(J) 31 (F)(G)(H)(J) 40 (A)(B)(C)(D) 49 (F)(G)(H)(J)
5 (A)(B)(C)(D) 14 (F)(G)(H)(J) 23 (A)(B)(C)(D) 32 (A)(B)(C)(D) 41 (F)(G)(H)(J) 50 (A)(B)(C)(D)
6 (F)(G)(H)(J) 15 (A)(B)(C)(D) 24 (F)(G)(H)(J) 33 (F)(G)(H)(J) 42 (A)(B)(C)(D) 51 (F)(G)(H)(J)
7 (A)(B)(C)(D) 16 (F)(G)(H)(J) 25 (A)(B)(C)(D) 34 (A)(B)(C)(D) 43 (F)(G)(H)(J) 52 (A)(B)(C)(D)
8 (F)(G)(H)(J) 17 (A)(B)(C)(D) 26 (F)(G)(H)(J) 35 (F)(G)(H)(J) 44 (A)(B)(C)(D) 53 (F)(G)(H)(J)
9 (A)(B)(C)(D) 18 (F)(G)(H)(J) 27 (A)(B)(C)(D) 36 (A)(B)(C)(D) 45 (F)(G)(H)(J)

TEST 2. Reading Comprehension

1 (A)(B)(C)(D) 7 (A)(B)(C)(D) 13 (A)(B)(C)(D) 19 (A)(B)(C)(D) 25 (A)(B)(C)(D) 31 (A)(B)(C)(D)
2 (F)(G)(H)(J) 8 (F)(G)(H)(J) 14 (F)(G)(H)(J) 20 (F)(G)(H)(J) 26 (F)(G)(H)(J) 32 (F)(G)(H)(J)
3 (A)(B)(C)(D) 9 (A)(B)(C)(D) 15 (A)(B)(C)(D) 21 (A)(B)(C)(D) 27 (A)(B)(C)(D) 33 (A)(B)(C)(D)
4 (F)(G)(H)(J) 10 (F)(G)(H)(J) 16 (F)(G)(H)(J) 22 (F)(G)(H)(J) 28 (F)(G)(H)(J) 34 (F)(G)(H)(J)
5 (A)(B)(C)(D) 11 (A)(B)(C)(D) 17 (A)(B)(C)(D) 23 (A)(B)(C)(D) 29 (A)(B)(C)(D)
6 (F)(G)(H)(J) 12 (F)(G)(H)(J) 18 (F)(G)(H)(J) 24 (F)(G)(H)(J) 30 (F)(G)(H)(J)

TEST 3. Spelling

1 (A)(B)(C)(D) 5 (A)(B)(C)(D) 9 (A)(B)(C)(D) 13 (A)(B)(C)(D) 17 (A)(B)(C)(D) 21 (A)(B)(C)(D)
2 (F)(G)(H)(J) 6 (F)(G)(H)(J) 10 (F)(G)(H)(J) 14 (F)(G)(H)(J) 18 (F)(G)(H)(J) 22 (F)(G)(H)(J)
3 (A)(B)(C)(D) 7 (A)(B)(C)(D) 11 (A)(B)(C)(D) 15 (A)(B)(C)(D) 19 (A)(B)(C)(D) 23 (A)(B)(C)(D)
4 (F)(G)(H)(J) 8 (F)(G)(H)(J) 12 (F)(G)(H)(J) 16 (F)(G)(H)(J) 20 (F)(G)(H)(J) 24 (F)(G)(H)(J)

TEST 4. Language Mechanics

1 Ⓐ Ⓑ Ⓒ Ⓓ	4 Ⓕ Ⓖ Ⓗ Ⓙ	7 Ⓐ Ⓑ Ⓒ Ⓓ	10 Ⓕ Ⓖ Ⓗ Ⓙ	13 Ⓐ Ⓑ Ⓒ Ⓓ	16 Ⓕ Ⓖ Ⓗ Ⓙ
2 Ⓕ Ⓖ Ⓗ Ⓙ	5 Ⓐ Ⓑ Ⓒ Ⓓ	8 Ⓕ Ⓖ Ⓗ Ⓙ	11 Ⓐ Ⓑ Ⓒ Ⓓ	14 Ⓕ Ⓖ Ⓗ Ⓙ	17 Ⓐ Ⓑ Ⓒ Ⓓ
3 Ⓐ Ⓑ Ⓒ Ⓓ	6 Ⓕ Ⓖ Ⓗ Ⓙ	9 Ⓐ Ⓑ Ⓒ Ⓓ	12 Ⓕ Ⓖ Ⓗ Ⓙ	15 Ⓐ Ⓑ Ⓒ Ⓓ	18 Ⓕ Ⓖ Ⓗ Ⓙ

TEST 5. Language Expression

1 Ⓐ Ⓑ Ⓒ Ⓓ	8 Ⓕ Ⓖ Ⓗ Ⓙ	15 Ⓐ Ⓑ Ⓒ Ⓓ	22 Ⓕ Ⓖ Ⓗ Ⓙ	29 Ⓐ Ⓑ Ⓒ Ⓓ	36 Ⓕ Ⓖ Ⓗ Ⓙ
2 Ⓕ Ⓖ Ⓗ Ⓙ	9 Ⓐ Ⓑ Ⓒ Ⓓ	16 Ⓕ Ⓖ Ⓗ Ⓙ	23 Ⓐ Ⓑ Ⓒ Ⓓ	30 Ⓕ Ⓖ Ⓗ Ⓙ	37 Ⓐ Ⓑ Ⓒ Ⓓ
3 Ⓐ Ⓑ Ⓒ Ⓓ	10 Ⓕ Ⓖ Ⓗ Ⓙ	17 Ⓐ Ⓑ Ⓒ Ⓓ	24 Ⓕ Ⓖ Ⓗ Ⓙ	31 Ⓐ Ⓑ Ⓒ Ⓓ	38 Ⓕ Ⓖ Ⓗ Ⓙ
4 Ⓕ Ⓖ Ⓗ Ⓙ	11 Ⓐ Ⓑ Ⓒ Ⓓ	18 Ⓕ Ⓖ Ⓗ Ⓙ	25 Ⓐ Ⓑ Ⓒ Ⓓ	32 Ⓕ Ⓖ Ⓗ Ⓙ	39 Ⓐ Ⓑ Ⓒ Ⓓ
5 Ⓐ Ⓑ Ⓒ Ⓓ	12 Ⓕ Ⓖ Ⓗ Ⓙ	19 Ⓐ Ⓑ Ⓒ Ⓓ	26 Ⓕ Ⓖ Ⓗ Ⓙ	33 Ⓐ Ⓑ Ⓒ Ⓓ	40 Ⓕ Ⓖ Ⓗ Ⓙ
6 Ⓕ Ⓖ Ⓗ Ⓙ	13 Ⓐ Ⓑ Ⓒ Ⓓ	20 Ⓕ Ⓖ Ⓗ Ⓙ	27 Ⓐ Ⓑ Ⓒ Ⓓ	34 Ⓕ Ⓖ Ⓗ Ⓙ	
7 Ⓐ Ⓑ Ⓒ Ⓓ	14 Ⓕ Ⓖ Ⓗ Ⓙ	21 Ⓐ Ⓑ Ⓒ Ⓓ	28 Ⓕ Ⓖ Ⓗ Ⓙ	35 Ⓐ Ⓑ Ⓒ Ⓓ	

TEST 6. Math Computation

1 Ⓐ Ⓑ Ⓒ Ⓓ Ⓔ	8 Ⓕ Ⓖ Ⓗ Ⓙ Ⓚ	15 Ⓐ Ⓑ Ⓒ Ⓓ Ⓔ	22 Ⓕ Ⓖ Ⓗ Ⓙ Ⓚ	29 Ⓐ Ⓑ Ⓒ Ⓓ Ⓔ	36 Ⓕ Ⓖ Ⓗ Ⓙ Ⓚ
2 Ⓕ Ⓖ Ⓗ Ⓙ Ⓚ	9 Ⓐ Ⓑ Ⓒ Ⓓ Ⓔ	16 Ⓕ Ⓖ Ⓗ Ⓙ Ⓚ	23 Ⓐ Ⓑ Ⓒ Ⓓ Ⓔ	30 Ⓕ Ⓖ Ⓗ Ⓙ Ⓚ	37 Ⓐ Ⓑ Ⓒ Ⓓ Ⓔ
3 Ⓐ Ⓑ Ⓒ Ⓓ Ⓔ	10 Ⓕ Ⓖ Ⓗ Ⓙ Ⓚ	17 Ⓐ Ⓑ Ⓒ Ⓓ Ⓔ	24 Ⓕ Ⓖ Ⓗ Ⓙ Ⓚ	31 Ⓐ Ⓑ Ⓒ Ⓓ Ⓔ	38 Ⓕ Ⓖ Ⓗ Ⓙ Ⓚ
4 Ⓕ Ⓖ Ⓗ Ⓙ Ⓚ	11 Ⓐ Ⓑ Ⓒ Ⓓ Ⓔ	18 Ⓕ Ⓖ Ⓗ Ⓙ Ⓚ	25 Ⓐ Ⓑ Ⓒ Ⓓ Ⓔ	32 Ⓕ Ⓖ Ⓗ Ⓙ Ⓚ	
5 Ⓐ Ⓑ Ⓒ Ⓓ Ⓔ	12 Ⓕ Ⓖ Ⓗ Ⓙ Ⓚ	19 Ⓐ Ⓑ Ⓒ Ⓓ Ⓔ	26 Ⓕ Ⓖ Ⓗ Ⓙ Ⓚ	33 Ⓐ Ⓑ Ⓒ Ⓓ Ⓔ	
6 Ⓕ Ⓖ Ⓗ Ⓙ Ⓚ	13 Ⓐ Ⓑ Ⓒ Ⓓ Ⓔ	20 Ⓕ Ⓖ Ⓗ Ⓙ Ⓚ	27 Ⓐ Ⓑ Ⓒ Ⓓ Ⓔ	34 Ⓕ Ⓖ Ⓗ Ⓙ Ⓚ	
7 Ⓐ Ⓑ Ⓒ Ⓓ Ⓔ	14 Ⓕ Ⓖ Ⓗ Ⓙ Ⓚ	21 Ⓐ Ⓑ Ⓒ Ⓓ Ⓔ	28 Ⓕ Ⓖ Ⓗ Ⓙ Ⓚ	35 Ⓐ Ⓑ Ⓒ Ⓓ Ⓔ	

TEST 7. Math Concepts and Applications

1 Ⓐ Ⓑ Ⓒ Ⓓ	9 Ⓐ Ⓑ Ⓒ Ⓓ	17 Ⓐ Ⓑ Ⓒ Ⓓ	25 Ⓐ Ⓑ Ⓒ Ⓓ	33 Ⓐ Ⓑ Ⓒ Ⓓ	41 Ⓐ Ⓑ Ⓒ Ⓓ
2 Ⓕ Ⓖ Ⓗ Ⓙ	10 Ⓕ Ⓖ Ⓗ Ⓙ	18 Ⓕ Ⓖ Ⓗ Ⓙ	26 Ⓕ Ⓖ Ⓗ Ⓙ	34 Ⓕ Ⓖ Ⓗ Ⓙ	42 Ⓕ Ⓖ Ⓗ Ⓙ
3 Ⓐ Ⓑ Ⓒ Ⓓ	11 Ⓐ Ⓑ Ⓒ Ⓓ	19 Ⓐ Ⓑ Ⓒ Ⓓ	27 Ⓐ Ⓑ Ⓒ Ⓓ	35 Ⓐ Ⓑ Ⓒ Ⓓ	43 Ⓐ Ⓑ Ⓒ Ⓓ
4 Ⓕ Ⓖ Ⓗ Ⓙ	12 Ⓕ Ⓖ Ⓗ Ⓙ	20 Ⓕ Ⓖ Ⓗ Ⓙ	28 Ⓕ Ⓖ Ⓗ Ⓙ	36 Ⓕ Ⓖ Ⓗ Ⓙ	44 Ⓕ Ⓖ Ⓗ Ⓙ
5 Ⓐ Ⓑ Ⓒ Ⓓ	13 Ⓐ Ⓑ Ⓒ Ⓓ	21 Ⓐ Ⓑ Ⓒ Ⓓ	29 Ⓐ Ⓑ Ⓒ Ⓓ	37 Ⓐ Ⓑ Ⓒ Ⓓ	45 Ⓐ Ⓑ Ⓒ Ⓓ
6 Ⓕ Ⓖ Ⓗ Ⓙ	14 Ⓕ Ⓖ Ⓗ Ⓙ	22 Ⓕ Ⓖ Ⓗ Ⓙ	30 Ⓕ Ⓖ Ⓗ Ⓙ	38 Ⓕ Ⓖ Ⓗ Ⓙ	46 Ⓕ Ⓖ Ⓗ Ⓙ
7 Ⓐ Ⓑ Ⓒ Ⓓ	15 Ⓐ Ⓑ Ⓒ Ⓓ	23 Ⓐ Ⓑ Ⓒ Ⓓ	31 Ⓐ Ⓑ Ⓒ Ⓓ	39 Ⓐ Ⓑ Ⓒ Ⓓ	47 Ⓐ Ⓑ Ⓒ Ⓓ
8 Ⓕ Ⓖ Ⓗ Ⓙ	16 Ⓕ Ⓖ Ⓗ Ⓙ	24 Ⓕ Ⓖ Ⓗ Ⓙ	32 Ⓕ Ⓖ Ⓗ Ⓙ	40 Ⓕ Ⓖ Ⓗ Ⓙ	48 Ⓕ Ⓖ Ⓗ Ⓙ

TEST 8. Reference and Study Skills

1 Ⓐ Ⓑ Ⓒ Ⓓ	6 Ⓕ Ⓖ Ⓗ Ⓙ	11 Ⓐ Ⓑ Ⓒ Ⓓ	16 Ⓕ Ⓖ Ⓗ Ⓙ	21 Ⓐ Ⓑ Ⓒ Ⓓ	26 Ⓕ Ⓖ Ⓗ Ⓙ
2 Ⓕ Ⓖ Ⓗ Ⓙ	7 Ⓐ Ⓑ Ⓒ Ⓓ	12 Ⓕ Ⓖ Ⓗ Ⓙ	17 Ⓐ Ⓑ Ⓒ Ⓓ	22 Ⓕ Ⓖ Ⓗ Ⓙ	27 Ⓐ Ⓑ Ⓒ Ⓓ
3 Ⓐ Ⓑ Ⓒ Ⓓ	8 Ⓕ Ⓖ Ⓗ Ⓙ	13 Ⓐ Ⓑ Ⓒ Ⓓ	18 Ⓕ Ⓖ Ⓗ Ⓙ	23 Ⓐ Ⓑ Ⓒ Ⓓ	28 Ⓕ Ⓖ Ⓗ Ⓙ
4 Ⓕ Ⓖ Ⓗ Ⓙ	9 Ⓐ Ⓑ Ⓒ Ⓓ	14 Ⓕ Ⓖ Ⓗ Ⓙ	19 Ⓐ Ⓑ Ⓒ Ⓓ	24 Ⓕ Ⓖ Ⓗ Ⓙ	29 Ⓐ Ⓑ Ⓒ Ⓓ
5 Ⓐ Ⓑ Ⓒ Ⓓ	10 Ⓕ Ⓖ Ⓗ Ⓙ	15 Ⓐ Ⓑ Ⓒ Ⓓ	20 Ⓕ Ⓖ Ⓗ Ⓙ	25 Ⓐ Ⓑ Ⓒ Ⓓ	30 Ⓕ Ⓖ Ⓗ Ⓙ

Vocabulary

This year you have an important kind of test to take. It's called a standardized test, and it's a special kind of multiple-choice test. The test you will take comes in eight parts. The first part tests your vocabulary, what you know about words.

Believe in yourself and don't worry. If you use the right strategies, you'll do a good job on every part of the test. A **strategy** is a plan for doing something. You employ strategies all the time. Do you roller blade? Here are two basic strategies you use to skate safely.

Strategy 1—Always wear a helmet, knee pads, and elbow pads.
Strategy 2—Skate on smooth, level ground.

Test-taking strategies show the same basic kind of common sense. And you master them the same way you master skating—by practice.

Learn About the Strategies

When you take the test, you have one goal. You want to give as many right answers as you can on each part of the test. To make this happen, pay attention to your coach's advice. Notice the three areas the strategies cover.

Time Strategies

- Work steadily. Don't stay too long on any one question.
- Skip difficult questions. Go back to them later.

I'm going to try my very best. I know I can do a good job.

Question Strategies

- Read the directions carefully. Then put the directions in your own words. Tell yourself what you need to do.
- Think of your own answers first. Then check for them in the choices.
- Think about the answer choices. Eliminate choices you know right off are wrong.

Answer Sheet Strategies

- When you go to mark the answer sheet, put your finger on the number of the question you're answering.
- Be sure to darken the correct circle. Read the letter inside.
- Darken only one answer circle for each question. Darken it completely.
- If you change an answer, erase your first answer completely.

Practice the Strategies

1. Identifying Words with Similar Meanings

Directions: Darken the circle for the word that has the <u>same</u> or <u>almost the same</u> meaning as the underlined word.

Sample A

<u>sudden</u> rain
A brief
B unexpected
C comfortable
D silly

What are the
directions telling
me to do?

I'll tell myself what the
underlined words mean.
Then I'll check the
answers.

1 rugged <u>terrain</u>
A planet
B sports
C animal
D ground

2 <u>expensive</u> gift
F beautiful
G costly
H thoughtful
J unclear

3 sweet <u>aroma</u>
A smell
B drink
C color
D taste

4 <u>spoiled</u> milk
F outdated
G sour
H musical
J tasty

5 <u>boisterous</u> crowd
A busy
B forgetful
C noisy
D illegal

6 quickly <u>harvest</u>
F gather
G display
H grow
J rename

7 <u>continuing</u> adventures
A timely
B ongoing
C wild
D funny

8 small <u>fragments</u>
F remarks
G clothes
H pieces
J bullets

9 <u>barren</u> land
A rainy
B gentle
C lifeless
D foreign

10 <u>unruly</u> passengers
F cowardly
G dreary
H clever
J rowdy

11 completely <u>shatter</u>
A find
B repair
C lose
D break

12 <u>gruesome</u> mask
F handsome
G ugly
H golden
J cheap

What is the
number of the
question I am
answering?

A Ⓐ Ⓑ Ⓒ Ⓓ
1 Ⓐ Ⓑ Ⓒ Ⓓ
2 Ⓕ Ⓖ Ⓗ Ⓙ

3 Ⓐ Ⓑ Ⓒ Ⓓ
4 Ⓕ Ⓖ Ⓗ Ⓙ
5 Ⓐ Ⓑ Ⓒ Ⓓ

6 Ⓕ Ⓖ Ⓗ Ⓙ
7 Ⓐ Ⓑ Ⓒ Ⓓ
8 Ⓕ Ⓖ Ⓗ Ⓙ

9 Ⓐ Ⓑ Ⓒ Ⓓ
10 Ⓕ Ⓖ Ⓗ Ⓙ
11 Ⓐ Ⓑ Ⓒ Ⓓ

12 Ⓕ Ⓖ Ⓗ Ⓙ

Answers: A B; 1 D; 2 G; 3 A; 4 G; 5 C; 6 F; 7 B; 8 H; 9 C; 10 J; 11 D; 12 G

2. Identifying Words with Opposite Meanings

Directions: Darken the circle for the word that has the <u>opposite</u> meaning as the underlined word.

Sample A

<u>bright</u> colors

A lively

B unfair

C dark

D paste

> Opposites are things like night and day.

> I won't waste time on a hard question. I'll skip to the next one.

1 something <u>whispered</u>
A created
B remembered
C shouted
D forbidden

2 <u>drab</u> clothing
F dreary
G dark
H thin
J colorful

3 quiet <u>murmur</u>
A puzzle
B shout
C freeze
D movement

4 something <u>frantic</u>
F calm
G sandy
H real
J healthful

5 <u>scatter</u> around
A complain
B annoy
C toss
D collect

6 amusing <u>conclusion</u>
F start
G middle
H ending
J bottom

7 something <u>narrow</u>
A wide
B stringy
C powerful
D locked

8 <u>bellow</u> loudly
F fight
G shout
H whisper
J stamp

9 <u>breakneck</u> speed
A watery
B stale
C rapid
D slow

10 something <u>temporary</u>
F breakable
G permanent
H tough
J responsible

11 move <u>forward</u>
A backward
B ahead
C beneath
D freely

12 something <u>modern</u>
F reliable
G fancy
H old-fashioned
J spoiled

> I have to darken each circle completely.

A Ⓐ Ⓑ Ⓒ Ⓓ   3 Ⓐ Ⓑ Ⓒ Ⓓ   6 Ⓕ Ⓖ Ⓗ Ⓙ   9 Ⓐ Ⓑ Ⓒ Ⓓ   12 Ⓕ Ⓖ Ⓗ Ⓙ
1 Ⓐ Ⓑ Ⓒ Ⓓ   4 Ⓕ Ⓖ Ⓗ Ⓙ   7 Ⓐ Ⓑ Ⓒ Ⓓ   10 Ⓕ Ⓖ Ⓗ Ⓙ
2 Ⓕ Ⓖ Ⓗ Ⓙ   5 Ⓐ Ⓑ Ⓒ Ⓓ   8 Ⓕ Ⓖ Ⓗ Ⓙ   11 Ⓐ Ⓑ Ⓒ Ⓓ

Answers: A C; 1 C; 2 J; 3 B; 4 F; 5 D; 6 F; 7 A; 8 H; 9 D; 10 G; 11 A; 12 H

3. Using Words With More Than One Meaning

Directions: Darken the circle for the word whose meaning fits both of the sentences.

Sample A

Spread the rug on the _____.
I saw the driver get into the car, _____the pedal, and leave at top speed.

  A flower
  B clobber
  C floor
  D pool

I'll look for clues in the sentences and find my own answers first.

STOP

Which answer choices can I forget about right away?

1 The old red barn had burned to the _____.
Scientists must _____ their beliefs in provable facts.

  A ground
  B level
  C plane
  D study

2 Plant the tulip bulbs in the flower _____.
If you're tired, go to _____ and get a good rest.

  F rift
  G vase
  H room
  J bed

3 He made a _____ and angry remark that he would soon regret.
Did you _____ to drop that glass?

  A nasty
  B mean
  C hurry
  D free

4 She struck a _____ to light the fire.
The soccer _____ between the two schools was postponed because of rain.

  F team
  G goal
  H match
  J ball

5 The owner tried to _____ the dog to do tricks. People who are unable to fly sometimes take the _____.

  A train
  B bribe
  C trust
  D plane

6 A _____ of questions entered my mind.
Water from the nearby _____ turns that water wheel.

  F lake
  G creek
  H pond
  J stream

STOP

I'll put my finger on the number of the question I'm answering.

A Ⓐ Ⓑ Ⓒ Ⓓ   2 Ⓕ Ⓖ Ⓗ Ⓙ   4 Ⓕ Ⓖ Ⓗ Ⓙ   6 Ⓕ Ⓖ Ⓗ Ⓙ
1 Ⓐ Ⓑ Ⓒ Ⓓ   3 Ⓐ Ⓑ Ⓒ Ⓓ   5 Ⓐ Ⓑ Ⓒ Ⓓ

Answers: A C; 1 A; 2 J; 3 B; 4 H; 5 A; 6 J

Practice the Strategies

4. Determining Word Origins

Directions: Darken the circle for the modern word whose meaning comes from the original word.

Sample A

Which word probably comes from the Latin word *planus*, meaning *flat, level*?

A planet
B plant
C plain
D pain

I'll look for a word that means the same thing as the word I'm being asked about.

STOP

I won't let myself get confused by sound-alike words. What's important is the meaning.

1 Which word probably comes from the Greek word *petalon*, meaning leaf?
A peddle
B petal
C paddle
D pet

2 Which word probably comes from the Old English word *deor*, meaning animal?
F deer
G door
H duty
J dear

3 Which word probably comes from the Greek word *akrobatos*, meaning *walking on tiptoe*?
A batter
B rubber
C across
D acrobat

4 Which word probably comes from the Spanish words *la reata* meaning *the rope*?
F rate
G lair
H lore
J lariat

5 Which word probably comes from the Chinese words *tai fung*, meaning *big wind*?
A fungus
B fun
C typoon
D type

6 Which word probably comes from the Latin word *cellarium*, meaning *storeroom*?
F sell
G alarm
H cellar
J cave

7 Which word probably comes from the French word *chaufer*, meaning *to warm*?
A charge
B chafe
C laugh
D change

8 Which word probably comes from the Latin word *mappa*, meaning *cloth*?
F ape
G map
H pappa
J mope

STOP

I'll make sure to darken the right letter.

A ⒶⒷⒸⒹ   2 ⒻⒼⒽⒿ   4 ⒻⒼⒽⒿ   6 ⒻⒼⒽⒿ   8 ⒻⒼⒽⒿ
1 ⒶⒷⒸⒹ   3 ⒶⒷⒸⒹ   5 ⒶⒷⒸⒹ   7 ⒶⒷⒸⒹ

Answers: A C; 1 B; 2 F; 3 D; 4 J; 5 C; 6 H; 7 B; 8 G

5. Understanding Words in Context

Directions: Darken the circle for the word that best completes the sentence.

Sample A

The room was _____ and needed a coat of paint.
Which word would indicate that the room is dark and dirty?

A dingy
B crabby
C content
D common

Before I look at the answers, I'll try to think of a word that fits.

STOP

The second sentence in the pair tells me the meaning of the word I need.

1 Al spoke in a soft, _____ voice that people could barely hear.
Which word would indicate that Al is shy or unsure of himself?

A bold
B loud
C forceful
D timid

2 Crossing a street can be _____ if you don't look both ways first.
Which word would indicate that crossing the street can be dangerous?

F harmless
G hazardous
H forcible
J fragile

3 My aunt _____ my family to visit her for the holidays.
Which word would indicate that the aunt asked the family to come where she lives?

A forced
B ordered
C invited
D improved

4 Many colorful birds flitted through the forest _____.
Which word indicate that the birds were flying through the top of the forest?

F canopy
G underbrush
H trees
J caves

5 The floor was so _____ that we could hear everyone's footsteps.
Which word would indicate that the floor made noises when people walked on it?

A cushioned
B hard
C wooden
D squeaky

6 Tom _____ a goal in the last minutes of the game, and his team won 2–1.
Which word would indicate that Tom made the winning goal?

F announced
G scored
H awarded
J blocked

STOP

I'll check my answers carefully.

A Ⓐ Ⓑ Ⓒ Ⓓ   2 Ⓕ Ⓖ Ⓗ Ⓙ   4 Ⓕ Ⓖ Ⓗ Ⓙ   6 Ⓕ Ⓖ Ⓗ Ⓙ
1 Ⓐ Ⓑ Ⓒ Ⓓ   3 Ⓐ Ⓑ Ⓒ Ⓓ   5 Ⓐ Ⓑ Ⓒ Ⓓ

Answers: A A; 1 D; 2 G; 3 C; 4 F; 5 D; 6 G

Vocabulary

Suggested time: 30 minutes

Read aloud to the class:

The questions on each part of the Vocabulary test are just like the questions you have been practicing.
Read the directions for each group of questions. Read the questions and the answer choices carefully. Then darken the circle for each correct answer. Keep working until you reach the word *STOP* at the bottom of page 21. Then put your pencil down.

For questions 1–12, darken the circle for the word that has the <u>same</u> or <u>almost the same</u> meaning as the underlined word.

1 often <u>recall</u>
  A repair
  B remember
  C leave
  D strike

2 sudden <u>commotion</u>
  F feeling
  G breeze
  H disturbance
  J music

3 fierce <u>blaze</u>
  A anger
  B animal
  C fire
  D hobby

4 <u>rival</u> team
  F opposite
  G friendly
  H unbeatable
  J jealous

5 <u>distant</u> thunder
  A real
  B loud
  C dangerous
  D far-off

6 <u>quiver</u> violently
  F shake
  G force
  H leap
  J shout

7 <u>complete</u> rest
  A endless
  B wise
  C miserable
  D total

8 <u>crisp</u> vegetables
  F cooked
  G soft
  H crunchy
  J healthful

9 three-car <u>collision</u>
  A race
  B crash
  C garage
  D repair

10 constantly <u>grumble</u>
  F great
  G explain
  H complain
  J roar

11 fancy <u>garb</u>
  A hair
  B clothing
  C curtains
  D car

12 <u>impressive</u> display
  F blunt
  G boring
  H heavy
  J exciting

GO ON ➡

1 Ⓐ Ⓑ Ⓒ Ⓓ   4 Ⓕ Ⓖ Ⓗ Ⓙ   7 Ⓐ Ⓑ Ⓒ Ⓓ   10 Ⓕ Ⓖ Ⓗ Ⓙ
2 Ⓕ Ⓖ Ⓗ Ⓙ   5 Ⓐ Ⓑ Ⓒ Ⓓ   8 Ⓕ Ⓖ Ⓗ Ⓙ   11 Ⓐ Ⓑ Ⓒ Ⓓ
3 Ⓐ Ⓑ Ⓒ Ⓓ   6 Ⓕ Ⓖ Ⓗ Ⓙ   9 Ⓐ Ⓑ Ⓒ Ⓓ   12 Ⓕ Ⓖ Ⓗ Ⓙ

Answers: 1 B; 2 H; 3 C; 4 F; 5 D; 6 F; 7 D; 8 H; 9 B; 10 H; 11 B; 12 J

For questions 13–27, darken the circle for the word that has the opposite meaning of the underlined word.

13 prompt arrival
   A lazy
   B new
   C bold
   D late

14 something imaginary
   F interesting
   G far-away
   H real
   J recent

15 retreat quickly
   A dig
   B attack
   C quit
   D leave

16 race ahead
   F leap
   G climb
   H speak
   J crawl

17 hilarious joke
   A humorous
   B serious
   C silly
   D unexpected

18 something remote
   F nearby
   G neglected
   H dangerous
   J unprepared

19 consume food
   A eat
   B remain
   C save
   D attack

20 careless error
   F grim
   G intentional
   H serious
   J unimportant

21 something rapid
   A fast
   B colorful
   C slow
   D lively

22 often permit
   F forbid
   G go
   H allow
   J follow

23 something obnoxious
   A pleasant
   B noisy
   C bothersome
   D grotesque

24 defend strongly
   F help
   G build
   H betray
   J belong

25 something joyful
   A delightful
   B incomplete
   C sad
   D sleepy

26 something hazardous
   F dangerous
   G safe
   H pleasant
   J breathtaking

27 build quickly
   A create
   B raise
   C shout
   D destroy

GO ON

13 Ⓐ Ⓑ Ⓒ Ⓓ   16 Ⓕ Ⓖ Ⓗ Ⓙ   19 Ⓐ Ⓑ Ⓒ Ⓓ   22 Ⓕ Ⓖ Ⓗ Ⓙ   25 Ⓐ Ⓑ Ⓒ Ⓓ
14 Ⓕ Ⓖ Ⓗ Ⓙ   17 Ⓐ Ⓑ Ⓒ Ⓓ   20 Ⓕ Ⓖ Ⓗ Ⓙ   23 Ⓐ Ⓑ Ⓒ Ⓓ   26 Ⓕ Ⓖ Ⓗ Ⓙ
15 Ⓐ Ⓑ Ⓒ Ⓓ   18 Ⓕ Ⓖ Ⓗ Ⓙ   21 Ⓐ Ⓑ Ⓒ Ⓓ   24 Ⓕ Ⓖ Ⓗ Ⓙ   27 Ⓐ Ⓑ Ⓒ Ⓓ

For questions 28–35, darken the circle for the word whose meaning fits both of the sentences.

28 The boss has the ____ to fire an employee. This dam makes many millions of watts of electrical ____.
  A right
  B power
  C thaw
  D reprimand

29 The settlers built a town on the left ____ of the river.
Keep your money in your piggy ____.
  F shore
  G jar
  H bank
  J bag

30 The ___ on the fence stated No Trespassing. Remember to ____ your name at the bottom of the letter.
  A field
  B sign
  C warning
  D notice

31 The drill is ____ a hole in a cement wall. The only thing on TV was a ____ show about politics.
  F making
  G creating
  H boring
  J stinging

32 A gift is something you get for ____. The children decided to ____ the bird when its wing was healed.
  A free
  B lend
  C nothing
  D freedom

33 George is such a ____ that he will do anything for a laugh.
Lunch is a ____ sandwich on a roll.
  F clown
  G slam
  H ham
  J jam

34 The plumber used a pump to ____ water from the basement.
Hair clogged the ____ in the sink.
  A outlet
  B drain
  C remove
  D faucet

35 The driver touched the gas ____ and moved the car into traffic.
How fast can you ____ your bike?
  F level
  G pedal
  H steer
  J jet

GO ON

28 Ⓐ Ⓑ Ⓒ Ⓓ   30 Ⓐ Ⓑ Ⓒ Ⓓ   32 Ⓐ Ⓑ Ⓒ Ⓓ   34 Ⓐ Ⓑ Ⓒ Ⓓ
29 Ⓕ Ⓖ Ⓗ Ⓙ   31 Ⓕ Ⓖ Ⓗ Ⓙ   33 Ⓕ Ⓖ Ⓗ Ⓙ   35 Ⓕ Ⓖ Ⓗ Ⓙ

Answers: 28 B; 29 H; 30 B; 31 H; 32 A; 33 H; 34 B; 35 G

For questions 36–45, darken the circle for the modern word whose meaning comes from the original word.

36 Which word probably comes from the Dutch word *baas*, meaning *master*?
- **A** butch
- **B** boss
- **C** busy
- **D** base

37 Which word probably comes from the Persian word *qand*, meaning *sugar*?
- **F** kind
- **G** hand
- **H** quote
- **J** candy

38 Which word probably comes from the Spanish words *el largato*, meaning *the lizard*?
- **A** large
- **B** gate
- **C** enlarge
- **D** alligator

39 Which word probably comes from the Italian word *traffico*, meaning *push, shove*?
- **F** traffic
- **G** fickle
- **H** raffle
- **J** trap

40 Which word probably comes from the French words *ma dame*, meaning *my lady*?
- **A** maid
- **B** mad
- **C** madam
- **D** dam

41 Which word probably comes from the French word *journee*, meaning *a day's travel*?
- **F** attorney
- **G** advent
- **H** journey
- **J** tournament

42 Which word probably comes from the Dutch word *hutselen*, meaning *to shake*?
- **A** hustle
- **B** harvest
- **C** harm
- **D** sell

43 Which word probably comes from the German word *Schnorchel*, meaning *nose*?
- **F** shore
- **G** snorkel
- **H** ignore
- **J** orchard

44 Which word probably comes from the Latin word *cava*, meaning *hollow*?
- **A** cause
- **B** vague
- **C** available
- **D** cave

45 Which word probably comes from the Old English word *ceap*, meaning *price, bargain*?
- **F** chief
- **G** cheap
- **H** cap
- **J** reap

GO ON

36 Ⓐ Ⓑ Ⓒ Ⓓ   38 Ⓐ Ⓑ Ⓒ Ⓓ   40 Ⓐ Ⓑ Ⓒ Ⓓ   42 Ⓐ Ⓑ Ⓒ Ⓓ   44 Ⓐ Ⓑ Ⓒ Ⓓ
37 Ⓕ Ⓖ Ⓗ Ⓙ   39 Ⓕ Ⓖ Ⓗ Ⓙ   41 Ⓕ Ⓖ Ⓗ Ⓙ   43 Ⓕ Ⓖ Ⓗ Ⓙ   45 Ⓕ Ⓖ Ⓗ Ⓙ

Answers: 36 B; 37 J; 38 D; 39 F; 40 C; 41 H; 42 A; 43 G; 44 D; 45 G

20

For questions 46–53, darken the circle for the word that best completes the sentence.

46 The divers could not see the shipwreck in the ____ waters of the bay.
Which word would indicate that the water in the bay was hard to see through?
  A clear
  B murky
  C calm
  D sparkling

47 The workers needed to ____ the damage caused by the flood.
Which word would indicate that the workers had to fix something?
  F investigate
  G count
  H repair
  J avoid

48 The ____ soup made Mavis feel that her tongue was on fire.
Which word would indicate that the soup was very spicy?
  A peppery
  B watery
  C dutiful
  D mild

49 Jeremy was ____ when he did not get the gift he wanted.
Which word would indicate that Jeremy was very sad?
  F angry
  G bold
  H heartbroken
  J difficult

50 Pat decided to ____ home rather than to drive to the city in snowy weather.
Which word would indicate that Pat decided to stay at home?
  A rush
  B remain
  C visit
  D complain

51 After the clean-up crew finished its job, the garden was ____.
Which word would indicate that the garden was spotless?
  F watered
  G swampy
  H empty
  J immaculate

52 Everyone felt ____ about the new plan and thought it would work.
Which word would indicate that everyone was strongly in favor of the new plan?
  A enthusiastic
  B upset
  C concerned
  D haphazard

53 Peggy ____ that her bike was better than everyone else's.
Which word would indicate that Peggy bragged about her bike?
  F instructed
  G bemoaned
  H boasted
  J complained

STOP

46 Ⓐ Ⓑ Ⓒ Ⓓ   48 Ⓐ Ⓑ Ⓒ Ⓓ   50 Ⓐ Ⓑ Ⓒ Ⓓ   52 Ⓐ Ⓑ Ⓒ Ⓓ
47 Ⓕ Ⓖ Ⓗ Ⓙ   49 Ⓕ Ⓖ Ⓗ Ⓙ   51 Ⓕ Ⓖ Ⓗ Ⓙ   53 Ⓕ Ⓖ Ⓗ Ⓙ

Test 2

Reading Comprehension

You've learned how to use strategies to answer vocabulary questions on tests. Now you'll learn strategies that will help you answer questions about reading passages. You'll also keep working on basic strategies you will need for every test.

Learn About the Strategies

A reading comprehension test tries to find out how much you understand what you read. You'll get a passage from a book. Then you'll get some questions about the passage.

Reading for a Purpose

You always have a purpose for reading. Sometimes you read for fun. Sometimes you read to find information—the score in a game or a famous actor's real name. Sometimes you read to collect facts you will put together with other facts in a report or for a debate.

Reading for a test isn't the same as reading on your own or in class. Your purpose for reading on the test is to answer the questions correctly. Listen to Coach TestWise's advice about reading passages.

> Read the questions first. Then read the passage carefully. Read to find answers to the questions.

> Don't let outside knowledge get in the way. Use only the information in the passage to answer the questions.

When to Use Background Knowledge

Another kind of reading question appears on the reading part of the test. This question asks you to use what you know from outside the test. Here are two of the kinds of things you'll be asked about.

Which of the following sentences states something that is a fact?	Which of the following sentences could be found in a story about a real person?

Here's what to do:

- Put the directions in your own words. Tell yourself what you need to do.

- Give yourself a real example before you start.

> "I like summer" is an opinion. "Summer is hot" is a fact.

> Stories about real people tell about things that could really happen, like fires and accidents.

6. Answering Questions about Reading Passages

Directions: Read the passage. Darken the circle for the correct answer to each question.

Sample A

Fishing equipment can be expensive or inexpensive. It depends on how much you have or want to spend. Most sporting goods stores have good fishing equipment for a reasonable price. But even with very little money to spend, you can get fishing equipment that will do the job.

This passage is mostly about

A the joy of fishing
B the cost of fishing equipment
C the kind of people who fish
D when people like to fish

Which answer choices can I eliminate right away?

 STOP

I need to read the questions before I read the passage.

The pinto is not a breed of horse, like the Shire and Falabella are. It is the name for a horse with black or brown and white markings. The word *pinto* comes from a Spanish word, *pintado*, which means "painted." Sometimes these horses are called paints.

Pintos were a favorite horse of the Indian tribes that lived in the western part of our country. The Indians liked to ride them when they went hunting, because the horses' coloring made them hard to see.

1 What is a pinto?

A a breed of horse
B a color of horse
C a Spanish horse
D an imaginary horse

2 A "paint" is

F a kind of pinto
G another name for pinto
H a pinto that is one color
J a very small pinto

3 Why did Indians like to ride pintos?

A Pintos were slow.
B Pintos liked to hunt.
C Pintos were tame and easy to ride.
D Pintos were hard to see.

4 Shires and Falabellas are

F Indian tribes
G parts of the country
H animals the Indians hunted
J breeds of horses

 STOP

I'll put my finger on the number of the question I'm answering.

A Ⓐ Ⓑ Ⓒ Ⓓ   2 Ⓕ Ⓖ Ⓗ Ⓙ   4 Ⓕ Ⓖ Ⓗ Ⓙ
1 Ⓐ Ⓑ Ⓒ Ⓓ   3 Ⓐ Ⓑ Ⓒ Ⓓ

Answers: A B; 1 B; 2 G; 3 D; 4 J

Three kinds of deer live in Yellowstone National Park. One species is called mule deer because they have long mule-like ears—even when they are young. Mule deer have antlers that are shed each winter and grow back during the summer.

The two other kinds of deer found in Yellowstone are moose and wapiti, or American elk. American elk are larger than mule deer and have dark hair on their necks. Moose are the largest members of the deer family. Their long legs help them to walk through deep snow or wade through streams.

Pronghorn antelope are also found in Yellowstone. They are well-suited to flat areas where there are few trees. Pronghorn have large eyes to see long distances and strong legs to run away from danger.

I'll remember to use *only* the facts I find in the passage.

5 Mule deer are so named because
  A they are stubborn like mules
  B they are not real deer
  C they carry heavy loads
  D they have long mule-like ears

6 In the first paragraph, what does "shed" mean?
  F a small building
  G dropped off
  H stock room
  J stored away

7 A wapiti is
  A another name for mule deer
  B a place in Yellowstone Park
  C an American elk
  D a moose

8 Which animal is the largest member of the deer family?
  F the moose
  G the American elk
  H the mule deer
  J the pronghorn antelope

9 What helps the moose cross streams?
  A its long legs
  B its fear of danger
  C its need to drink
  D its antlers

10 What is this passage mostly about?
  F mule deer
  G moose
  H pronghorn antelope
  J the deer of Yellowstone

11 Which word best describes a pronghorn's eyesight?
  A weak
  B sharp
  C tiny
  D narrow

12 What kind of ground are pronghorn antelope best suited to?
  F very hilly ground
  G mountaintops
  H flat, treeless ground
  J swampy ground

STOP

Am I putting my answer next to the right number?

5 Ⓐ Ⓑ Ⓒ Ⓓ 7 Ⓐ Ⓑ Ⓒ Ⓓ 9 Ⓐ Ⓑ Ⓒ Ⓓ 11 Ⓐ Ⓑ Ⓒ Ⓓ
6 Ⓕ Ⓖ Ⓗ Ⓙ 8 Ⓕ Ⓖ Ⓗ Ⓙ 10 Ⓕ Ⓖ Ⓗ Ⓙ 12 Ⓕ Ⓖ Ⓗ Ⓙ

Answers: 5 D; **6** G; **7** C; **8** F; **9** A; **10** J; **11** B; **12** H

Enjoyed all over the world, volleyball is an inexpensive, fun sport. It can be played indoors or outdoors. Volleyball can be a serious, competitive sport or a game played just for fun without paying strict attention to the rules. One reason volleyball is so popular is that it is basically a very simple game. All you really have to do is hit a ball back and forth over a net and keep the ball from touching the ground on your side.

Another reason for volleyball's popularity is that almost anyone can play the game and play it fairly well with just a little practice. You don't have to be tall, strong, or fast to play volleyball. Volleyball players come in all shapes, sizes, and ages.

Because volleyball doesn't need much special equipment, it is a perfect game to play at the beach, at a picnic, or in a gym during winter. So whatever the season is, you can always enjoy the game of volleyball.

> Should I skip any question and go back to it later?

13 Where is volleyball played?
A only in the United States
B only in Europe
C only in Africa
D everywhere in the world

14 Which word best describes the kind of game volleyball is?
F rule-filled
G lonely
H simple
J complicated

15 What is the main thing a person needs in order to be a good volleyball player?
A speed
B height
C practice
D physical strength

16 In the first paragraph, a competitive sport is a sport
F played on the beach
G played to win, as pro teams play
H played in all seasons
J played for fun

17 When can people play volleyball?
A only in the summer
B only in the winter
C all year round
D in the spring and fall

18 Besides a ball, what other piece of equipment does volleyball need?
F bats
G special shoes
H a helmet
J a net

19 If the other team is serving, what do you think happens if the ball touches the ground on your side of the net?
A The other team scores a point.
B Both teams score a point.
C The game ends.
D The teams shake hands.

20 What is this passage mostly about?
F the rules of volleyball
G different types of volleyball
H the popularity of volleyball
J the history of volleyball

STOP

> If I skipped a question, did I leave a place for the answer?

13 Ⓐ Ⓑ Ⓒ Ⓓ   15 Ⓐ Ⓑ Ⓒ Ⓓ   17 Ⓐ Ⓑ Ⓒ Ⓓ   19 Ⓐ Ⓑ Ⓒ Ⓓ
14 Ⓕ Ⓖ Ⓗ Ⓙ   16 Ⓕ Ⓖ Ⓗ Ⓙ   18 Ⓕ Ⓖ Ⓗ Ⓙ   20 Ⓕ Ⓖ Ⓗ Ⓙ

Answers: 13 D; 14 H; 15 C; 16 G; 17 C; 18 J; 19 A; 20 H

Like snakes, lizards, and crocodiles, turtles are *reptiles*. These are egg-laying, cold- blooded animals whose body temperature stays about the same as their surroundings. In cold weather, they have a hard time keeping warm and active. That's why turtles, like all reptiles, cannot live in areas that are cold year-round. (Human beings are warm-blooded and so can live in cold climates throughout the year.)

Turtles are the only reptiles with shells. Most of them can pull the head, legs, and tail inside the shell as protection against enemies. Turtles live in deserts, forests, lakes, marshes, prairies, meadows, and the sea. Some are dangerous, but most are harmless.

Finding land-dwelling turtles is usually a matter of luck. They like moist, open woods or swamps. Water turtles are easier to see. If you walk quietly and look carefully along a wide stream, river, or pond, you will probably see some turtles. Turtles like to climb up on rocks, floating logs, and dense sea plants to sun themselves.

Turtles do not have teeth, but they do have horny bills that can tear up plant and animal food. Turtles eat worms, bugs, fish, shellfish, grubs, and plants.

I only have to read the questions, not the answer choices, before I read the passage.

21 What does a turtle's body temperature control?
  A how much the turtle weighs
  B how big the turtle can grow
  C how active the turtle can be
  D what the turtle likes to eat

22 Why can't turtles live in places that are cold year-round?
  F They melt in the cold.
  G They are cold-blooded.
  H No one feeds them when its cold.
  J They have many enemies there.

23 Where do turtles live?
  A only on land
  B only in the water
  C only in deserts
  D almost everywhere

24 Why do turtles like to climb up on rocks?
  F to play slide-off games
  G to look for prey
  H to scratch their stomachs
  J to sun themselves

25 What makes a turtle special among reptiles?
  A It has legs.
  B It lays eggs.
  C It is cold-blooded.
  D It has a shell.

26 What does the turtle probably use its shell for?
  F decoration
  G protection
  H storage
  J frustration

27 Which body feature do turtles not have?
  A tails
  B shells
  C teeth
  D horny bills

28 What is this passage about?
  F where to look for turtles
  G how turtles swim
  H feeding turtles
  J why turtles have shells

Did I darken only one circle on each line?

| 21 | Ⓐ Ⓑ Ⓒ Ⓓ | 23 | Ⓐ Ⓑ Ⓒ Ⓓ | 25 | Ⓐ Ⓑ Ⓒ Ⓓ | 27 | Ⓐ Ⓑ Ⓒ Ⓓ |
| 22 | Ⓕ Ⓖ Ⓗ Ⓙ | 24 | Ⓕ Ⓖ Ⓗ Ⓙ | 26 | Ⓕ Ⓖ Ⓗ Ⓙ | 28 | Ⓕ Ⓖ Ⓗ Ⓙ |

Answers: 21 C; **22** G; **23** D; **24** J; **25** D; **26** G; **27** C; **28** F

7. Answering Reading Questions

Directions: Darken the circle for the sentence that best answers the question.

Sample A

Which of the following sentences is probably from a story?
A Lincoln was born in 1809.
B The peace treaty was signed in 1945.
C The Iroquois Indians sided with the British during the Revolutionary War.
D The doorbell rang, and in walked Bruno wearing a football helmet.

What kind of sentence
would I expect to find
in a story?
Events should seem made up.

STOP

I'll read each question
and all answer choices.
I'll look for clues.

1 Which of the following sentences could **not** be based on fact?
A December 21 is the shortest day of the year.
B Suddenly, the magician laughed shrilly, and flames burst from his fingertips.
C There are three kinds of hockey—ice hockey, roller hockey, and field hockey.
D The bicycle racers swooped down main street and turned at City Hall.

2 Which of the following sentences states the writer's opinion about something?
F Cocoa is an ingredient in chocolate ice cream.
G Ticket prices are higher this year than last year.
H The blue whale is larger than any dinosaur that ever lived.
J Mariah Kelly is the best candidate for mayor.

3 Which of the following sentences is probably from a biography?
A Before the days of steam, sailing ships carried people to every part of the world.
B A large shopping mall will open on Highway 5 next year.
C The 1960s were an exciting time for a musician to be born.
D High up in the sky, the hawk spotted its prey and began to circle.

4 Which of the following sentences could be the last sentence in a story about dogs?
F The fallen tree looked heavy—too heavy to move without help.
G There were no clouds in the sky the day Clem's adventure began.
H Clem wagged his tail as if to say, "We made it. We survived."
J The bear was of average size, but an average-sized bear is bigger than a dog.

STOP

If I changed an answer,
did I erase the old
answer completely?

A Ⓐ Ⓑ Ⓒ Ⓓ   2 Ⓕ Ⓖ Ⓗ Ⓙ   4 Ⓕ Ⓖ Ⓗ Ⓙ
1 Ⓐ Ⓑ Ⓒ Ⓓ   3 Ⓐ Ⓑ Ⓒ Ⓓ

Answers: A D; 1 B; 2 J; 3 C; 4 H

Reading Comprehension

Suggested time: 40 minutes

Read aloud to the class:

The questions on each part of the Reading Comprehension test are just like the questions you have been practicing.

Read the directions for each group of questions. Read the questions and the answer choices carefully. Then darken the circle for each correct answer. Keep working until you reach the word *STOP* at the bottom of page 32. Then put your pencil down.

For questions 1–28, darken the circle for the correct answer to each question.

What is the most popular sport in the world? Did you guess soccer? If you did, you're right! Soccer is played and loved by millions of fans all over the globe.

In many countries, soccer is called football. "Football" is a good name for this sport. That's because to play soccer, a player must use his or her feet.

How did soccer become the world's most popular sport? It is a long story that begins more than two thousand years ago. Soccer was played by the ancient Greeks and Romans. It was also played in one form or another by the Chinese, the Japanese, and the Aztec Indians.

1 In the first paragraph, what does "fan" mean?
  A a machine that makes air move
  B enthusiastic follower
  C player
  D coach

2 What is another name for soccer in some countries?
  F football
  G basketball
  H tennis
  J handball

3 According to the passage, which of these statements is true about soccer?
  A It is almost as popular as baseball.
  B It is the world's most popular sport.
  C People first played soccer in 1910.
  D The Aztecs invented soccer.

4 What is this passage mostly about?
  F how soccer got its name
  G the popularity of soccer
  H the rules for soccer
  J soccer fans

GO ON →

---

1 Ⓐ Ⓑ Ⓒ Ⓓ   3 Ⓐ Ⓑ Ⓒ Ⓓ
2 Ⓕ Ⓖ Ⓗ Ⓙ   4 Ⓕ Ⓖ Ⓗ Ⓙ

Answers: 1 B; 2 F; 3 B; 4 G

Crayfish are small crustaceans (water creatures that usually have some kind of shell) that look like tiny lobsters. They live in brooks, creeks, and the shallow parts of streams, rivers, and ponds. Crayfish can be as tiny as the tip of your pinky or as large as your biggest finger. Finding and catching crayfish can be lots of fun.

To catch crayfish, you can use a cup, a bucket, an old can, or just your hand. Crayfish have claws resembling pincers, but they cannot squeeze your skin hard enough to hurt. So do not be afraid to handle them.

Crayfish like to hide under rocks in the water. Walk along the stream slowly, turning over stones in the water as you do. Wait for the rising cloud of mud to clear. Look in the water where you turned over the stone. You may see a crayfish crawling along the bottom.

Crayfish swim backward very quickly in spurts. To catch one, hold a cup, can, or your hand behind the crayfish's tail. Put your other hand in the water, moving it toward the front of the crayfish. The crayfish will be frightened and swim backward into the cup or can. Quickly lift up the cup to prevent it from swimming out.

5 Where do crayfish live?
- **A** in the ocean
- **B** in buckets and old cans
- **C** in clouds of mud
- **D** in brooks and shallow streams

6 How do most crustaceans differ from other water creatures?
- **F** They have gills.
- **G** They have fins on their backs.
- **H** They have shells.
- **J** They cannot swim.

7 The largest crayfish is as large as
- **A** a fingertip
- **B** a finger
- **C** a hand
- **D** an arm

8 According to the passage, which statement about crayfish is true?
- **F** It does not hide from predators.
- **G** It makes a good pet.
- **H** It swims slowly.
- **J** It has claws like pincers.

9 In the first paragraph, what does "shallow" mean?
- **A** cold
- **B** fast-moving
- **C** not deep
- **D** murky

10 Where are you most likely to find a crayfish?
- **F** underwater under a rock
- **G** on land, near a tree
- **H** swimming on the surface
- **J** leaping from the water into the air

11 In the last paragraph, what does "spurts" mean?
- **A** wavy motions
- **B** short bursts
- **C** muddy steps
- **D** long leaps

12 What is this passage mostly about?
- **F** how to catch crayfish
- **G** how to eat crayfish
- **H** how crayfish survive in the wild
- **J** the crayfish's natural enemies

GO ON

5 Ⓐ Ⓑ Ⓒ Ⓓ   7 Ⓐ Ⓑ Ⓒ Ⓓ   9 Ⓐ Ⓑ Ⓒ Ⓓ   11 Ⓐ Ⓑ Ⓒ Ⓓ
6 Ⓕ Ⓖ Ⓗ Ⓙ   8 Ⓕ Ⓖ Ⓗ Ⓙ   10 Ⓕ Ⓖ Ⓗ Ⓙ   12 Ⓕ Ⓖ Ⓗ Ⓙ

Answers: 5 D; 6 H; 7 B; 8 J; 9 C; 10 F; 11 B; 12 F

A calorie is the measure of energy produced by food. Calories are needed for fuel and used up during workouts. Everyone burns or uses calories at a different rate. That is why some people can eat a lot and stay thin, while others eat the same amount and gain weight.

It takes 3,500 calories to make one pound of body weight. If you take in 7,000 calories and only burn up 3,500 calories, you will gain a pound. That is the real secret to losing or gaining weight.

The food you eat has calories. The exercise you do burns up a number of calories. If you use up 3,500 more calories than you take in, you will lose a pound. If you use up the same number of calories you take in, your weight will stay the same.

When you are working out, don't be afraid to drink water. It will help replace fluids lost while sweating, and it won't increase your weight.

13 What does a calorie measure?
  A body temperature
  B the amount of fat in body cells
  C the energy it takes to eat food
  D the energy made by food

14 How many calories does the body need to make one pound of body weight?
  F 1,500
  G 3,500
  H 7,000
  J 10,000

15 According to the passage, why can some people eat a lot and stay thin?
  A They sometimes skip meals.
  B They eat vegetable.
  C They burn calories at a fast rate.
  D They exercise less.

16 Where do people get calories?
  F from food
  G from exercise
  H from the air
  J from body weight

17 According to the passage, how does exercise affect weight loss?
  A It keeps you busy.
  B It burns calories.
  C It makes up for overeating.
  D It gives you a reason to drink water.

18 According to the passage, how does a person lose weight?
  F by not eating desserts
  G by eating more calories than you burn
  H by eating fewer calories than you burn
  J by overeating and working out

19 In the last paragraph, what does "fluids" mean?
  A nourishment
  B food solids
  C liquids in the body
  D refreshment

20 What is this passage mostly about?
  F eating low-fat foods
  G how to exercise properly
  H going on a diet
  J what calories are

GO ON

13 Ⓐ Ⓑ Ⓒ Ⓓ   15 Ⓐ Ⓑ Ⓒ Ⓓ   17 Ⓐ Ⓑ Ⓒ Ⓓ   19 Ⓐ Ⓑ Ⓒ Ⓓ
14 Ⓕ Ⓖ Ⓗ Ⓙ   16 Ⓕ Ⓖ Ⓗ Ⓙ   18 Ⓕ Ⓖ Ⓗ Ⓙ   20 Ⓕ Ⓖ Ⓗ Ⓙ

Answers: 13 D; 14 G; 15 C; 16 F; 17 B; 18 H; 19 C; 20 J

Watching a skilled gymnast perform is a thrilling sight. Gymnasts gracefully flip, spin, balance, and fly through the air. To be a gymnast, you have to have strength, flexibility, agility, coordination, courage, and plenty of determination.

Why do you need determination? A gymnast is not the kind of athlete who gives up easily. A gymnastic routine that takes only minutes to perform often takes hundreds of hours of practice to master. Many times a gymnast practices the same maneuver over and over again until it can be done flawlessly. That is why a gymnast must be a determined and devoted athlete.

But gymnastics is not all work and no play. It is really lots of fun to do. Gymnastics also helps you build self-confidence and stay physically fit.

21 In the passage above, what does "determination" mean?
- **A** firm resolve
- **B** confidence
- **C** patience
- **D** choppiness

22 Why do gymnasts need determination?
- **F** Not many people are interested.
- **G** Routines are simple but long.
- **H** Routines take hours to master.
- **J** Audiences don't attend rehearsals.

23 According to the passage, how long does it take a gymnast to perform a routine?
- **A** a few minutes
- **B** an hour
- **C** a few hours
- **D** a day

24 In paragraph two, which word could the writer use in place of "maneuver"?
- **F** skill
- **G** courage
- **H** practice
- **J** movement

25 In paragraph two, what does "flawlessly" mean?
- **A** without complaint
- **B** without mistakes
- **C** without fear
- **D** without support

26 How do you think gymnasts feel after they master a routine?
- **F** upset with themselves
- **G** proud of themselves
- **H** sorry they began gymnastics
- **J** ready to try a different sport

27 How does knowing that you have the skill to do something well make you feel?
- **A** self-confident
- **B** sore
- **C** uncertain
- **D** self-conscious

28 What is this passage mostly about?
- **F** what it takes to be a gymnast
- **G** girls' gymnastics
- **H** physical fitness
- **J** how to get started in gymnastics

GO ON ➤

21 Ⓐ Ⓑ Ⓒ Ⓓ   23 Ⓐ Ⓑ Ⓒ Ⓓ   25 Ⓐ Ⓑ Ⓒ Ⓓ   27 Ⓐ Ⓑ Ⓒ Ⓓ
22 Ⓕ Ⓖ Ⓗ Ⓙ   24 Ⓕ Ⓖ Ⓗ Ⓙ   26 Ⓕ Ⓖ Ⓗ Ⓙ   28 Ⓕ Ⓖ Ⓗ Ⓙ

Answers: 21 A; 22 H; 23 A; 24 J; 25 B; 26 G; 27 A; 28 F

For questions 29–34, darken the circle for the sentence that best answers each question.

29 Which of the following phrases or sentences would you expect to find in a letter?
   A Follow the directions to assemble the bicycle.
   B The judge asked the jury if it had reached a verdict in the case.
   C Sincerely yours
   D A tall stranger entered and sat at a table.

30 Which of the following sentences states a fact?
   F Computers are fun to use.
   G Computers will someday run the world.
   H The letters WWW stand for World Wide Web.
   J All your friends will envy you if have this video game.

31 Which of the following statements from an editorial states an opinion?
   A The city should not allow the park to become a parking lot.
   B Local store owners want the city to make Platte Park into a parking lot.
   C The mayor and store owners have not reached an agreement.
   D Platte Park reopened in 1990.

32 Which of the following sentences could be the closing sentence of a story about two friends?
   F Sue turned, waved for the last time, and climbed into her family's car.
   G This comment made Veronica feel all the more stubborn.
   H Sue met Veronica on their first day in kindergarten.
   J "Sue, I can't find the map you put back in the drawer."

33 Which of the following sentences is probably from a book of nonfiction?
   A Scientists once again think that dinosaurs were cold-blooded.
   B The moon seemed to follow me as I walked down the block.
   C Jess always wanted to be an astronaut, and now she was captain of the space shuttle.
   D The tired little mouse stopped for a snack.

34 Once upon a time there were two sisters. This statement would probably be found in
   F a tall tale
   G a biography
   H a fairy tale
   J a biography

---

29 Ⓐ Ⓑ Ⓒ Ⓓ   31 Ⓐ Ⓑ Ⓒ Ⓓ   33 Ⓐ Ⓑ Ⓒ Ⓓ
30 Ⓕ Ⓖ Ⓗ Ⓙ   32 Ⓕ Ⓖ Ⓗ Ⓙ   34 Ⓕ Ⓖ Ⓗ Ⓙ

Test 3
Spelling

Using test-taking strategies is just like practicing any other skill. The more you practice, the better you get. As you work through this part of *TestWise*, you'll learn how to apply strategies to the spelling test.

Learn About the Strategies

One part of the spelling test tries to find out if you can recognize words that are spelled correctly. The other part has you recognize words that are spelled incorrectly. The spelling test, like the others you've practiced for, is multiple choice. Only one of the four answer choices is the right answer.

Question Strategy

Read the directions carefully.
Then put the directions in your own words.
Tell yourself what you need to do.

Spelling Strategies

- Look for words inside words.
- Stretch out words to hear all the sounds in the word
- Use spelling rules
    1. the *i* before *e* rule
       fierce   neighbor

    2. the final *e* rule
       fake/faked

    3. the *y* to *i* rule
       fancy/fanciful

    4. the *f* to *v* rule
       leaf/leaves

    5. The final consonant rule
       pan/panning

Always be sure you know what you're looking for. Are you looking for a misspelled word or a correctly spelled word? Use the question strategy I showed you.

Don't get confused by looking at lots of misspelled words. Before you study the choices, decide for yourself how a word should be spelled.

Use the spelling strategies you have learned in school to help you pick correctly spelled words.

Finally, always be sure to darken the correct circle when you record your answer.

8. Finding the Correct Spelling

Directions: Darken the circle for the word that is spelled correctly.

Sample A

We used a rake to gather the ____.
A leavz
B leafs
C leaves
D leeves

> First, how would I spell the word?

STOP

> I'll read each question and *all* answer choices. I will look for clues.

1 Only a few ____ of bread were left.
A crums
B crumz
C crumbs
D crummbs

2 The guide was ____ that we could find the path.
F hopful
G hoppful
H hoapful
J hopeful

3 My dog ____ almost sixty pounds.
A weighs
B weights
C weize
D whays

4 We have not ____ the people who helped us.
F forgoten
G foregotten
H forgotn
J forgotten

5 The family lived ____ ever after.
A happily
B happly
C happyly
D hapily

6 Tickets for the ____ are very expensive.
F consert
G concirt
H concert
J koncirt

7 The cook served waffles for ____ .
A brekfast
B breekfast
C breakfes
D breakfast

8 There are two ____ and a horse in the barn.
F dunkees
G donkeys
H donkies
J dunkeys

9 Have you ever visited a ____ country?
A foren
B forn
C foreign
D forign

STOP

> Did I darken the correct circle?

A Ⓐ Ⓑ Ⓒ Ⓓ	2 Ⓕ Ⓖ Ⓗ Ⓙ	4 Ⓕ Ⓖ Ⓗ Ⓙ	6 Ⓕ Ⓖ Ⓗ Ⓙ	8 Ⓕ Ⓖ Ⓗ Ⓙ
1 Ⓐ Ⓑ Ⓒ Ⓓ	3 Ⓐ Ⓑ Ⓒ Ⓓ	5 Ⓐ Ⓑ Ⓒ Ⓓ	7 Ⓐ Ⓑ Ⓒ Ⓓ	9 Ⓐ Ⓑ Ⓒ Ⓓ

Answers: A C; 1 C; 2 J; 3 A; 4 J; 5 A; 6 H; 7 D; 8 G; 9 C

9. Finding the Incorrect Spelling

Directions: Darken the circle for the group of words in which the underlined word is <u>not</u> spelled correctly.

Sample A

   A make a <u>guess</u>
   B a <u>taistee</u> treat
   C a <u>broken</u> promise
   D the <u>route</u> to my house

I'll remember to look for the word that's *not* spelled right.

I'll read *all* the answer choices and look for clues.

1 **A** a bushel of <u>peeches</u>
     B an <u>oak</u> tree
     C <u>helpful</u> advice
     D an <u>armful</u> of twigs

2 **F** the <u>famous</u> musician
     G a <u>forbiden</u> food
     H a <u>graceful</u> runner
     J a speedy <u>automobile</u>

3 **A** a <u>powerful</u> computer
     B a <u>roal</u> of clear tape
     C an Italian <u>restaurant</u>
     D an art <u>museum</u>

4 **F** a fancy <u>necktie</u>
     G a <u>roomful</u> of friends
     H a <u>goald</u> necklace
     J a <u>loaf</u> of bread

5 **A** a <u>freezing</u> day
     B a violent <u>tyfoon</u>
     C a <u>magic</u> trick
     D a <u>necessary</u> warning

6 **F** a friendly <u>nieghborhood</u>
     G a <u>mysterious</u> stranger
     H an <u>honest</u> mistake
     J a complete <u>surprise</u>

7 **A** a <u>shining</u> example
     B a proud <u>proclamation</u>
     C a loud <u>complante</u>
     D a <u>loud</u> gong

8 **F** a <u>steep</u> hill
     G a <u>noble</u> deed
     H a drop in the <u>temperachure</u>
     J <u>deep</u> trouble

Darken the circle completely

A Ⓐ Ⓑ Ⓒ Ⓓ   2 Ⓕ Ⓖ Ⓗ Ⓙ   4 Ⓕ Ⓖ Ⓗ Ⓙ   6 Ⓕ Ⓖ Ⓗ Ⓙ   8 Ⓕ Ⓖ Ⓗ Ⓙ
1 Ⓐ Ⓑ Ⓒ Ⓓ   3 Ⓐ Ⓑ Ⓒ Ⓓ   5 Ⓐ Ⓑ Ⓒ Ⓓ   7 Ⓐ Ⓑ Ⓒ Ⓓ

Answers: A B; 1 A; 2 G; 3 B; 4 H; 5 B; 6 F; 7 C; 8 H

Spelling

Suggested time: 20 minutes

Read aloud to the class:

The questions on each part of the Spelling test are just like the questions you have been practicing.

Read the directions for each group of questions. Read the questions and the answer choices carefully. Then darken the circle for each correct answer. Keep working until you reach the word *STOP* at the bottom of page 37. Then put your pencil down.

For questions 1–12, darken the circle for the word that is spelled correctly.

1 The baker made twenty ____ of bread.
A loves
B looves
C loaves
D loavz

2 When does ____ vacation start?
F summer
G soamer
H soamer
J sumer

3 The lake water was ____ clear.
A cristal
B cristle
C crystle
D crystal

4 In this cave you can hear your voice ____ .
F ecco
G echo
H ecko
J eko

5 I was ____ when I slipped and fell into the water.
A midstreem
B middstream
C midstream
D midstreme

6 A ____ of apples fell from the truck.
F crat
G craet
H creat
J crate

7 These ____ are no longer in style.
A close
B clooze
C cloaze
D clothes

8 The team ____ the captain to help them win.
F beaged
G begged
H beged
J begd

9 The ____ carried the bag of baseball bats.
A coch
B coach
C coache
D coatch

10 The first-prize ____ will be notified by mail.
F whinner
G winner
H winer
J winnr

11 Ten cents is a ____ price to pay for a book.
A cheap
B chepe
C cheape
D chep

12 There is heavy ____ during rush hour.
F trafeck
G trafick
H traffic
J traffik

GO ON

1 Ⓐ Ⓑ Ⓒ Ⓓ 4 Ⓕ Ⓖ Ⓗ Ⓙ 7 Ⓐ Ⓑ Ⓒ Ⓓ 10 Ⓕ Ⓖ Ⓗ Ⓙ
2 Ⓕ Ⓖ Ⓗ Ⓙ 5 Ⓐ Ⓑ Ⓒ Ⓓ 8 Ⓕ Ⓖ Ⓗ Ⓙ 11 Ⓐ Ⓑ Ⓒ Ⓓ
3 Ⓐ Ⓑ Ⓒ Ⓓ 6 Ⓕ Ⓖ Ⓗ Ⓙ 9 Ⓐ Ⓑ Ⓒ Ⓓ 12 Ⓕ Ⓖ Ⓗ Ⓙ

Answers: 1 C; 2 F; 3 D; 4 G; 5 C; 6 J; 7 D; 8 G; 9 B; 10 G; 11 A; 12 H

For questions 13–24, darken the circle for the group of words in which the underlined word is not spelled correctly.

13
A a <u>lively</u> party
B a <u>convenient</u> location
C a <u>nastey</u> comment
D an <u>underground</u> stream

14
F a real <u>privlege</u>
G a <u>hospital</u> volunteer
H silly <u>gossip</u>
J wiped out the <u>disease</u>

15
A a <u>narrow</u> escape
B <u>green</u> hills
C a <u>cotton</u> shirt
D two lively <u>monkies</u>

16
F two sharp <u>knives</u>
G out of <u>focus</u>
H a <u>regretible</u> mistake
J a new <u>vacuum</u> cleaner

17
A a <u>greasy</u> floor
B a glowing <u>candle</u>
C a litter of <u>puppys</u>
D a heavy <u>hammer</u>

18
F a warning <u>shout</u>
G <u>calm</u> feeling
H a tape <u>reccording</u>
J weak <u>eyesight</u>

19
A a <u>sudden</u> storm
B thin <u>trousers</u>
C The Atlantic <u>Oshean</u>
D a box of <u>matches</u>

20
F total <u>quiet</u>
G <u>selfish</u> behavior
H a bronze <u>statchew</u>
J <u>steady</u> speed

21
A a newspaper <u>article</u>
B the <u>loacal</u> post office
C the <u>astonished</u> newcomer
D a <u>wool</u> jacket

22
F a <u>mizerable</u> cold
G dear <u>diary</u>
H <u>solid</u> wood
J a <u>loose</u> collar

23
A an <u>astonnishing</u> excuse
B a <u>dangerous</u> street
C a metal <u>canoe</u>
D <u>messy</u> work

24
F a colorful <u>garden</u>
G the star's <u>autograph</u>
H a <u>comfortabel</u> sofa
J a <u>thorough</u> cleaning

STOP

13 Ⓐ Ⓑ Ⓒ Ⓓ   16 Ⓕ Ⓖ Ⓗ Ⓙ   19 Ⓐ Ⓑ Ⓒ Ⓓ   22 Ⓕ Ⓖ Ⓗ Ⓙ
14 Ⓕ Ⓖ Ⓗ Ⓙ   17 Ⓐ Ⓑ Ⓒ Ⓓ   20 Ⓕ Ⓖ Ⓗ Ⓙ   23 Ⓐ Ⓑ Ⓒ Ⓓ
15 Ⓐ Ⓑ Ⓒ Ⓓ   18 Ⓕ Ⓖ Ⓗ Ⓙ   21 Ⓐ Ⓑ Ⓒ Ⓓ   24 Ⓕ Ⓖ Ⓗ Ⓙ

© 1998 by Troll Communications L.L.C.

Answers: 13 C; 14 F; 15 D; 16 H; 17 C; 18 H; 19 C; 20 H; 21 B; 22 F; 23 A; 24 H

Language Mechanics

Language Mechanics means using capital letters and punctuation marks correctly in sentences. In this part of TestWise, you'll learn how to apply test-taking strategies to the capitalization and punctuation tests.

Learn About the Strategies

The formats of the tests in this part are a little different from the formats of the tests you've taken up to this point. Look carefully to see how answer choices are given. On both tests, one of the choices is None. Be on your guard. You aren't just looking for wrong answers. None means that the sentence is correct as it stands.

The Capitalization Test

On the capitalization test you need to decide where, if anywhere, in the sentence there is a mistake.

Check in these spots for capitalization mistakes

- the first word in a sentence
    Let's go home.
- the first word in a sentence that starts a quotation
    Jill said, "**T**hrow me the ball."
- where you see the word *I* or the actual name of a person, a place, or a thing.

    Marie **C**urie   **S**an **F**rancisco
    the **D**eclaration of **I**ndependence

The Punctuation Test

On the punctuation part, the best strategy is to proofread each question sentence. Find the problem (if there is one) in the sentence before you look at the answer choices.

- Check end punctuation. Be sure a sentence ends with a period, a question mark, or an exclamation mark.
- Be sure you understand why each punctuation mark in dark type is needed in these sentences.

    Yes**,** Pat**,** we have apples**,** peaches**,** and watermelon**,** but no one brought the ripe**,** juicy berries**.**

    My sister**,** the president of her class**,** said**,** **"**Vote for me for school senate.**"**

    Because he was in a rush**,** Al didn't have time to read Mavis**'s** report**,** Joan**'s** story**,** or the twins**'** rough draft.

10. Using Correct Capitalization

Directions: Darken the circle for the part of the sentence that needs a capital letter. Darken the circle for <u>None</u> if no capital letter is needed.

Sample A

On thursday	the whole school visited	the Milton Museum of Art.	
A	**B**	**C**	**D** None

I will read the whole sentence first.

STOP

I will try to find the mistake on my own first.

1 In early December | i read the funniest book | called Nasty, Stinky Sneakers.
   A | **B** | **C** | **D** None

2 Robert Frost is the poet | who wrote the poem | "Whose Woods These Are."
   F | **G** | **H** | **J** None

3 The students | in Sarah J. hale Middle School | are proud of their school.
   A | **B** | **C** | **D** None

4 During our summer vacation | we visited | Fargo, north dakota.
   F | **G** | **H** | **J** None

5 My mother | went to aunt Sally's | house for lunch yesterday,
   A | **B** | **C** | **D** None

6 All my friends | went to see a movie | while I was home sick.
   F | **G** | **H** | **J** None

7 On a trip to New York, | the baseball fans in the class | visited Yankee stadium.
   A | **B** | **C** | **D** None

8 Jeff asked, | "where do we keep | the children's books?"
   F | **G** | **H** | **J** None

I must completely erase any answers I change.

STOP

A (A)(B)(C)(D)   2 (F)(G)(H)(J)   4 (F)(G)(H)(J)   6 (F)(G)(H)(J)   8 (F)(G)(H)(J)
1 (A)(B)(C)(D)   3 (A)(B)(C)(D)   5 (A)(B)(C)(D)   7 (A)(B)(C)(D)

Answers: A A; 1 B; 2 J; 3 B; 4 H; 5 B; 6 J; 7 C; 8 G

11. Using Correct Punctuation

Directions: Darken the circle for the punctuation mark that would make the sentence correct. Darken the circle for <u>None</u> if no other punctuation mark is needed.

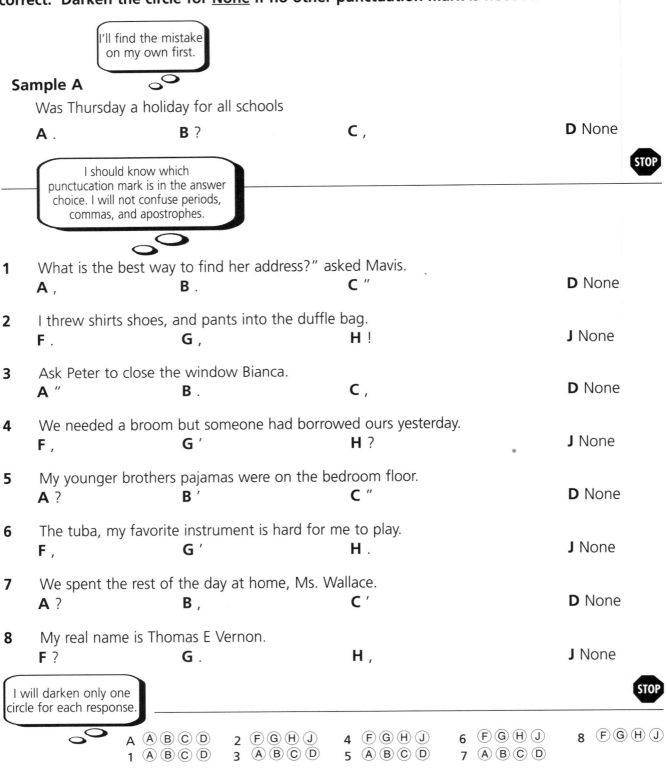

I'll find the mistake on my own first.

Sample A

Was Thursday a holiday for all schools

A .   **B** ?   **C** ,   **D** None

STOP

I should know which punctucation mark is in the answer choice. I will not confuse periods, commas, and apostrophes.

1   What is the best way to find her address?" asked Mavis.
A ,   **B** .   **C** "   **D** None

2   I threw shirts shoes, and pants into the duffle bag.
F .   **G** ,   **H** !   **J** None

3   Ask Peter to close the window Bianca.
A "   **B** .   **C** ,   **D** None

4   We needed a broom but someone had borrowed ours yesterday.
F ,   **G** '   **H** ?   **J** None

5   My younger brothers pajamas were on the bedroom floor.
A ?   **B** '   **C** "   **D** None

6   The tuba, my favorite instrument is hard for me to play.
F ,   **G** '   **H** .   **J** None

7   We spent the rest of the day at home, Ms. Wallace.
A ?   **B** ,   **C** '   **D** None

8   My real name is Thomas E Vernon.
F ?   **G** .   **H** ,   **J** None

STOP

I will darken only one circle for each response.

A Ⓐ Ⓑ Ⓒ Ⓓ   2 Ⓕ Ⓖ Ⓗ Ⓙ   4 Ⓕ Ⓖ Ⓗ Ⓙ   6 Ⓕ Ⓖ Ⓗ Ⓙ   8 Ⓕ Ⓖ Ⓗ Ⓙ
1 Ⓐ Ⓑ Ⓒ Ⓓ   3 Ⓐ Ⓑ Ⓒ Ⓓ   5 Ⓐ Ⓑ Ⓒ Ⓓ   7 Ⓐ Ⓑ Ⓒ Ⓓ

Answers: A B; 1 C; 2 G; 3 C; 4 F; 5 B; 6 F; 7 D; 8 G

Timed Practice Test/Use the Strategies on Your Own

Language Mechanics

Suggested time: 20 minutes

Read aloud to the class:

The questions on each part of the Language Mechanics test are just like the questions you have been practicing.
    Read the directions for each group of questions. Read the questions and the answer choices carefully. Then darken the circle for each correct answer. Keep working until you reach the word *STOP* at the bottom of page 42. Then put your pencil down.

For numbers 1–8, darken the circle for the part of the sentence that needs a capital letter. Darken the circle for <u>None</u> if no capital letter is needed.

1   the actor who played | Drake in the movie | has a fine voice.
        A   **B**   **C**   **D** None

2   Make a turn when you see | the sign at the corner | of President street.
        F   **G**   **H**   **J** None

3   My family always has | a family reunion on the last saturday | in May.
        A   **B**   **C**   **D** None

4   The famous Gateway Arch | is in the city | of st. Louis, Missouri.
        F   **G**   **H**   **J** None

5   is Peru | a country in | South America?
        A   **B**   **C**   **D** None

6   In the movie | a deadly missile | hits washington, D.C.
        F   **G**   **H**   **J** None

7   The small bridge over the highway | was covered with ice | from the storm.
        A   **B**   **C**   **D** None

8   A large portion | of this island was destroyed | by hurricane Norman.
        F   **G**   **H**   **J** None

1 Ⓐ Ⓑ Ⓒ Ⓓ   3 Ⓐ Ⓑ Ⓒ Ⓓ   5 Ⓐ Ⓑ Ⓒ Ⓓ   7 Ⓐ Ⓑ Ⓒ Ⓓ
2 Ⓕ Ⓖ Ⓗ Ⓙ   4 Ⓕ Ⓖ Ⓗ Ⓙ   6 Ⓕ Ⓖ Ⓗ Ⓙ   8 Ⓕ Ⓖ Ⓗ Ⓙ

Answers: 1 A; 2 H; 3 B; 4 H; 5 A; 6 H; 7 D; 8 H

For numbers 9–18, darken the circle for the punctuation mark that would make the sentence correct. Darken the circle for <u>None</u> if no other punctuation mark is needed.

9   New Orleans, Louisiana is at the mouth of the Mississippi River.
    A .   **B** ,   **C** "   **D** None

10   Books records, and tapes were on sale at the store.
    F '   **G** ,   **H** ?   **J** None

11   These are my books about my favorite detective Encyclopedia Brown.
    A ?   **B** ,   **C** "   **D** None

12   We needed a video camera some tapes, and a script.
    F ?   **G** ,   **H** !   **J** None

13   Marthas greeting card got lost in the mail.
    A '   **B** ,   **C** ?   **D** None

14   When did you know you had made a wrong turn
    F ,   **G** ?   **H** .   **J** None

15   I lost all the money I had one dollar.
    A .   **B** ,   **C** '   **D** None

16   What a terrific way to end the parade
    F ?   **G** .   **H** !   **J** None

17   Two dogs, a cat, and a hamster were for sale.
    A ,   **B** '   **C** .   **D** None

18   A bully is often not a brave person.
    F ,   **G** .   **H** "   **J** None

---

9   Ⓐ Ⓑ Ⓒ Ⓓ   11   Ⓐ Ⓑ Ⓒ Ⓓ   13   Ⓐ Ⓑ Ⓒ Ⓓ   15   Ⓐ Ⓑ Ⓒ Ⓓ   17   Ⓐ Ⓑ Ⓒ Ⓓ
10   Ⓕ Ⓖ Ⓗ Ⓙ   12   Ⓕ Ⓖ Ⓗ Ⓙ   14   Ⓕ Ⓖ Ⓗ Ⓙ   16   Ⓕ Ⓖ Ⓗ Ⓙ   18   Ⓕ Ⓖ Ⓗ Ⓙ

Answers: 9 B; 10 G; 11 B; 12 G; 13 A; 14 G; 15 B; 16 H; 17 D; 18 J

Language Expression

The Language Expression part of the test explores how well you can recognize good English. Questions test the right way to use words, form sentences, and create paragraphs. In this part of *TestWise*, you will learn more test-taking strategies. They will help you sharpen your ability to handle questions about using language.

Learn About the Strategies

The Usage Part

Some of the Language Expression questions test your language sense. They test if you can tell correct English and incorrect English apart. The English it tests you on is standard English. This is the kind of English you learn in school.

> All you need to know is that something's wrong. You don't need to know why it's wrong.

Question Strategy

Read all the choices carefully. Look for the choice you know is correct. Don't waste time figuring out why the other choices are incorrect.

These are some of the language problems you may find.

Incorrect	Correct	Incorrect	Correct
He ain't got	He doesn't have	There isn't no milk.	There isn't any milk. There is no milk
We seen him.	We saw him.	between you and I	between you and me
It's the bestest.	It's the best.	You and me are here.	You and I are here.
the tallest twin	The taller twin	Al he is strong.	Al is strong.
We is here.	We are here.	I fell. And hurt myself.	I fell and hurt myself.
Jo and Tad lives here.	Jo and Tad live here.	We rested. Because we were tired.	We rested because we were tired.

The Paragraph Part

Other parts of the Language Expression test explore if you know what makes a paragraph work. Questions will ask you to pick topic sentences, supporting sentences, and concluding sentences.

Question Strategy

After you make your choice, test it. Read the paragraph again with your choice in place. Decide if the paragraph makes sense.

12. Determining Usage

Directions: Darken the circle for the word or words that best complete each sentence.

Sample A

Peanuts is the ____ dog in the entire dog show.
- **A** heavier
- **B** most heaviest
- **C** most heavier
- **D** heaviest

I should look for the best answer in standard English.

STOP

I won't waste time figuring out why the wrong answers are wrong.

1 The bus driver told ____ that the gas tank was empty.
- **A** ourselves
- **B** we
- **C** us
- **D** myself

2 Yesterday I ____ my lunch to school in my new thermal lunch box.
- **F** bringed
- **G** brought
- **H** bring
- **J** brings

3 Jill travels to school the ____ way she can find.
- **A** most fastest
- **B** faster
- **C** fast
- **D** fastest

4 The school bell ____ too early yesterday morning, and everyone was late.
- **F** ringed
- **G** rung
- **H** rang
- **J** ringing

5 The librarian lent copies of the book to Jessica and ____.
- **A** me
- **B** my
- **C** I
- **D** myself

6 Everyone ____ waiting for the concert to begin tonight.
- **F** is
- **G** are
- **H** be
- **J** were

STOP

If I change an answer, I have to erase my old answer completely.

A Ⓐ Ⓑ Ⓒ Ⓓ   2 Ⓕ Ⓖ Ⓗ Ⓙ   4 Ⓕ Ⓖ Ⓗ Ⓙ   6 Ⓕ Ⓖ Ⓗ Ⓙ
1 Ⓐ Ⓑ Ⓒ Ⓓ   3 Ⓐ Ⓑ Ⓒ Ⓓ   5 Ⓐ Ⓑ Ⓒ Ⓓ

Answers: A D; 1 C; 2 G; 3 D; 4 H; 5 A; 6 F

13. Identifying Correct Usage

Directions: Darken the circle for the sentence that is written correctly.

Sample A

A   Waiting outside the theater.
B   The line stretched around the block.
C   Alice and me wait.
D   Cars honks their horns.

I notice that the directions say "sentence." The right answer has to be a complete sentence in standard English.

STOP

I'll look for the choice I know is right.

1   A   Where be a public telephone?
　　B   Looking down the street.
　　C   I found a phone in the drugstore.
　　D   Dad and me will be late for dinner.

2   F   We have two goat and five sheeps.
　　G   I wake up more earlier than she does.
　　H   The rooster wake up everyone.
　　J   We make the wool into cloth.

3   A   He hate to play chess.
　　B   Pat and me joined the tournament.
　　C   I enjoy checkers more than chess.
　　D   Playing chess well.

4   F   A new store is opening soon.
　　G   The old building burnded down.
　　H   The police didn't have no clue.
　　J   The fire blazing for hours.

5   A   He and I enjoys sports.
　　B   Playing soccer in the spring.
　　C   We play basketball indoors.
　　D   Is any sport more slower than baseball?

6   F   There is two projects I want to do.
　　G   We ain't got time for both projects.
　　H   They told Phyllis and I the price.
　　J   Three dollars is a low price.

7   A   We broke the box when we lifted it.
　　B   Bill he doesn't know his own strength.
　　C   We finded the box in the basement.
　　D   Are there a name on the box?

8   F   The ants invades our picnic.
　　G   It rained brief last night.
　　H   The ground should be dry.
　　J   Puddles is everywhere you can see.

STOP

A Ⓐ Ⓑ Ⓒ Ⓓ　　2 Ⓕ Ⓖ Ⓗ Ⓙ　　4 Ⓕ Ⓖ Ⓗ Ⓙ　　6 Ⓕ Ⓖ Ⓗ Ⓙ　　8 Ⓕ Ⓖ Ⓗ Ⓙ
1 Ⓐ Ⓑ Ⓒ Ⓓ　　3 Ⓐ Ⓑ Ⓒ Ⓓ　　5 Ⓐ Ⓑ Ⓒ Ⓓ　　7 Ⓐ Ⓑ Ⓒ Ⓓ

Answers: A B; 1 C; 2 J; 3 C; 4 F; 5 C; 6 J; 7 A; 8 H

14. Combining Sentences

Directions: Darken the circle for the sentence that best combines the two sentences.

Sample A

The children wore sweaters.

The children wore heavy coats

A The sweater children wore heavy coats.
B The children wearing sweaters wore heavy coats.
C The heavy children wore coats and sweaters.
D The children wore sweaters and heavy coats.

I'll think of my own answers first. I don't want to be confused by all the choices.

The new sentence should have the same meaning as the two separate sentences.

1 Jessica hit the ball.
The ball broke a window.
A Jessica broke a window and hit the ball.
B The ball that Jessica hit broke a window.
C Jessica hit a window and broke the ball.
D The ball broke a window, but Jessica hit the ball.

2 Min bought a pair of leather boots.
The boots are very fashionable.
F Min bought a pair of leather boots that are very fashionable.
G Fashionable Min bought a pair of leather boots.
H Min bought a leather, fashionable pair of boots.
J The boots are fashionable and leather and they belong to Min.

3 The Hawks received the first-place trophy.
They won every game.
A The Hawks received every game and won the first-place trophy.
B The Hawks who received the first-place trophy they also won every game.
C The Hawks received the first-place trophy because they won every game.
D The Hawks received the first-place trophy until they won every game.

4 We were stranded by the roadside.
The tow truck came.
F The roadside stranded us until the tow truck came.
G We were stranded by the roadside until the tow truck came.
H We and the tow truck were stranded by the roadside.
J The tow truck stranded us by the roadside.

I'll darken only one circle next to a number.

A Ⓐ Ⓑ Ⓒ Ⓓ   2 Ⓕ Ⓖ Ⓗ Ⓙ   4 Ⓕ Ⓖ Ⓗ Ⓙ
1 Ⓐ Ⓑ Ⓒ Ⓓ   3 Ⓐ Ⓑ Ⓒ Ⓓ

Answers: A D; 1 B; 2 F; 3 C; 4 G

15. Choosing Topic Sentences

Directions: Darken the circle for the topic sentence that best fits each paragraph.

Sample A

_____. You need to give them food and water every day. You need to clean where they live, too. If you have trained your rabbit to use a litter box, you should remove soiled litter every day. You should change soiled bedding in its box, or hutch, every day, as well.

A Rabbits are fun house pets.
B Rabbits come in many colors.
C Rabbits and hares are different animals.
D Rabbits need daily care.

A topic sentence tells what the main idea of the paragraph is.

STOP

I'll make my choice. Then read the paragraph again, with my choice in place.

1 _____. These bikes have fat, knobby tires that grip the road. They have flat handlebars that let the rider sit upright. They have sturdy frames and sometimes even shock absorbers. These bikes can take a beating.

A There are two types of bikes that people ride.
B Handlebars are a bike's most important feature.
C Mountain bikes are designed for unpaved ground.
D Riders of all ages enjoy biking.

2 _____. Hockey skates have smooth, curved blades. Figure skates have flat blades. The blades on hockey skates help the skater make quick, fast turns to follow the puck. The blade of a figure skate ends in a toe pick. The toe pick helps the skater stop and do spins.

F Anyone can learn to figure skate.
G Speed skaters have special blades on their skates, too.
H Hockey skates and figure skates have special purpose blades.
J Hockey is a fast and dangerous sport.

STOP

I'll be sure to darken the circle completely.

A Ⓐ Ⓑ Ⓒ Ⓓ   2 Ⓕ Ⓖ Ⓗ Ⓙ
1 Ⓐ Ⓑ Ⓒ Ⓓ

Answers: A D; 1 C; 2 H

16. Recognizing Supporting Details

Directions: Darken the circle for the choice that gives the best supporting details to develop the topic sentence.

Sample A

Giraffes are plant eaters.

Supporting sentences give details that explain the topic sentence.

A A giraffe's long neck lets it spot predators while they are still far away. It can gallop as fast as thirty miles an hour for short distances.

B I like to go to the zoo and watch the giraffes. They're very interesting creatures to watch.

C A young giraffe is too short to reach the tender leaves at the top of a tree. Its mother may pick a bunch of tender leaves from the top of the tree for her baby to eat.

D The life span of a giraffe is fifteen to twenty years. Giraffes rarely have twins.

STOP

I'll think about the topic sentence. What details might I add? Then read the choices.

1 Some birds are unable to fly.

A Some seabirds such as the albatross have long, graceful wings. Their wings let them soar through the air for hours.

B Many species of birds fly south for winter. They often travel in flocks.

C Penguins and ostriches have very small wings. Their wings could never lift them off the ground.

D It is only a story that frightened ostriches bury their heads in the sand. They run away or kick at enemies with their strong legs.

2 Whales are the largest creatures that ever lived.

F Whales don't have gills like fish. They have lungs. Whales have to return to the surface to breathe.

G Fish move by wiggling their tails from side to side. Whales push themselves forward by moving their tails up and down.

H Most whales are larger than elephants. The largest whale, the blue whale, is bigger than the largest dinosaur.

J Some whales can stay underwater for over an hour. These are whales that dive very deep.

3 A tiger's stripes have many uses.

A Tigers are not like most cats. For one thing, tigers like to swim. Swimming keeps them cool.

B They help the tiger hide in grass. They also help us tell tigers apart. No two tigers have the same pattern of stripes.

C Tiger cubs start to learn how to hunt when they are about six months old.

D Tigers are solitary animals. This means that they like to be by themselves.

STOP

I'll be sure to darken the circle completely.

A Ⓐ Ⓑ Ⓒ Ⓓ   2 Ⓕ Ⓖ Ⓗ Ⓙ
1 Ⓐ Ⓑ Ⓒ Ⓓ   3 Ⓐ Ⓑ Ⓒ Ⓓ

Answers: A C; 1 C; 2 H; 3 B

48

17. Finding Sentences That Do Not Belong

Directions: Darken the circle for the sentence that does <u>not</u> belong in the paragraph.

Sample A

¹The cheetah is the fastest animal on land. ²Mountain lions run fast, too. ³In short bursts, a cheetah can run more than sixty miles an hour. ⁴It stalks its prey slowly and then races from its hiding place to make the kill.

A sentence 1   **C** sentence 3

B sentence 2   **D** sentence 4

I notice that each sentence in the paragraph has a number.

STOP

I'll make my choice. Then I'll read the paragraph again, with my choice in place.

1   ¹Seals are excellent swimmers. ²Their bullet-shaped bodies and their flippers help them move through water swiftly. ³You can tell seals and sea lions apart because sea lions have visible ears. ⁴The Weddell seal can stay underwater for seventy minutes and dive as deep as two thousand feet.

A sentence 1   **C** sentence 3

B sentence 2   **D** sentence 4

2   ¹Automobiles were once called horseless carriages. ²The Morgan horse is one of the most popular breeds of horse in the United States. ³Morgans have great speed and strength. ⁴Morgans are used for riding, racing, and pulling light loads.

F sentence 1   **H** sentence 3

G sentence 2   **J** sentence 4

3   ¹A porcupine's quills protect it from enemies. ²These quills are hollow, hooked spines that cover the animal's sides, back, and tail. ³If an attacker touches the quills, they stick in the attacker's skin. ⁴Skunks use their scent glands for protection.

A sentence 1   **C** sentence 3

B sentence 2   **D** sentence 4

STOP

A Ⓐ Ⓑ Ⓒ Ⓓ   2 Ⓕ Ⓖ Ⓗ Ⓙ

1 Ⓐ Ⓑ Ⓒ Ⓓ   3 Ⓐ Ⓑ Ⓒ Ⓓ

Answers: A B; 1 C; 2 F; 3 D

17. Completing Paragraphs

Directions: Darken the circle for the sentence that best completes the paragraph.

Sample A

The Arctic tundra is a frozen, treeless land. The snowy owl is one of the few birds that live in the tundra. Owls usually hunt only at night. But in the Arctic the sun does not set all summer long. _____.

A Birds that hunt at night are called nocturnal.
B Permafrost is permanently frozen soil below the surface.
C A snowy owl's feathers are white.
D The snowy owl must hunt its prey in the daylight.

I will read each paragraph twice. I will tell myself what the main idea is.

 STOP

I need to be sure that the ending works with the rest of the paragraph.

1 Roadrunners are not just cartoon birds. They're real, and they love to run. They seldom fly. Instead, they rely on their swiftness of foot to catch the lizards, mice, and snakes they usually eat. They can race as fast as fifteen miles per hour on their long, spindly legs. _____.
A Like all birds, roadrunners are hatched from eggs.
B Roadrunners are members of the cuckoo family.
C Its feathers are brown, streaked with white.
D Their speed can also help them reach safety if a predator appears.

2 A horned toad is actually a member of the lizard family. It is not a toad at all. What look like horns on the sides and back of its head are really spiny scales. It has sharp claws on its toes, but it mostly lives on the ground. When it's frightened by an attacker, it buries itself in the soil or squirts blood from special sacs under its eyes. _____.
F Lizards are cold-blooded.
G The squirts of blood may also scare the attacker away.
H Some lizards can lose their tails.
J Maybe birds like to attack them.

STOP

A Ⓐ Ⓑ Ⓒ Ⓓ   2 Ⓕ Ⓖ Ⓗ Ⓙ
1 Ⓐ Ⓑ Ⓒ Ⓓ

Answers: A D; 1 D; 2 G

Language Expression

Suggested time: 40 minutes

Read aloud to the class:

The questions on each part of the Language Expression test are just like the questions you have been practicing.

Read the directions for each group of questions. Read the questions and the answer choices carefully. Then darken the circle for each correct answer. Keep working until you reach the word *STOP* at the bottom of page 57. Then put your pencil down.

For numbers 1–6, darken the circle for the word or words that best complete each sentence.

1 Leo and _____ carried the drum set home from the music store.
- **A** me
- **B** myself
- **C** I
- **D** mine

2 In the race between the tortoise and the hare, which animal ran _____?
- **F** slower
- **G** the slowest
- **H** the most slowly
- **J** slowliest

3 We dressed _____ in our fanciest clothes for the party.
- **A** us
- **B** usselves
- **C** ourselves
- **D** ours

4 Yesterday I _____ that I would never find my lost scarf.
- **F** thinked
- **G** thoughted
- **H** thank
- **J** thought

5 My poor, sick dog is feeling _____ today than yesterday.
- **A** betterer
- **B** better
- **C** weller
- **D** more better

6 Do not clean the camera lens _____ than you need to, or you may scratch it.
- **F** more oftener
- **G** most often
- **H** most oftenest
- **J** more often

GO ON ➡

1 Ⓐ Ⓑ Ⓒ Ⓓ   3 Ⓐ Ⓑ Ⓒ Ⓓ   5 Ⓐ Ⓑ Ⓒ Ⓓ
2 Ⓕ Ⓖ Ⓗ Ⓙ   4 Ⓕ Ⓖ Ⓗ Ⓙ   6 Ⓕ Ⓖ Ⓗ Ⓙ

Answers: 1 C; 2 F; 3 C; 4 J; 5 B; 6 J

For numbers 7–18, darken the circle for the sentence that is written correctly.

7   A   Because they stopped early.
       B   They were sudden quiet.
       C   The door opened with a creak.
       D   Scaring us silly.

8   F   To ride safely.
       G   Always wearing a helmet.
       H   Buy a tire pump for your bike.
       J   I don't have no money for a pump.

9   A   Rabbits appeal to Jess and I.
       B   Raising rabbits is fun.
       C   A buck and a doe.
       D   Baby rabbits are born laterer at night.

10   F   This jet is the most fastest aircraft here.
       G   My uncle he enjoys air shows.
       H   Because my aunt likes flying, too.
       J   I like to watch stunt flying.

11   A   Hanging posters in my room.
       B   I painted the walls light blue.
       C   I like that color the mostest of all.
       D   Even though the paint spilled.

12   F   We bringed our books to the library.
       G   Because the line was very long.
       H   The librarian recommends this book.
       J   The librarian and me are friends.

13   A   Today is Jan's birthday.
       B   Silly to make a fuss.
       C   We gived her a surprise party.
       D   Blowing out candles and making a wish.

14   F   An invitation to a costume party.
       G   Us friends went as a group.
       H   We had the bestest time ever.
       J   We wore scary masks.

15   A   Trained for the school marathon.
       B   The runners practicing in the park.
       C   They jogged every day.
       D   Chris ran more fastly than Pam.

16   F   Swimming lessons at the pool.
       G   The group played water polo.
       H   Hitting the ball to a teammate.
       J   Mandy scored the firstest goal.

17   A   We seen the birds in the nest.
       B   The nest was outside my window.
       C   The little birds they were always hungry.
       D   Flew back with food for the baby birds.

18   F   We eated the apples, plums, and pears.
       G   The pears were the most juiciest fruits.
       H   The plums had purple skins.
       J   They saved the berries for Anne and I.

GO ON

7 Ⓐ Ⓑ Ⓒ Ⓓ   10 Ⓕ Ⓖ Ⓗ Ⓙ   13 Ⓐ Ⓑ Ⓒ Ⓓ   16 Ⓕ Ⓖ Ⓗ Ⓙ
8 Ⓕ Ⓖ Ⓗ Ⓙ   11 Ⓐ Ⓑ Ⓒ Ⓓ   14 Ⓕ Ⓖ Ⓗ Ⓙ   17 Ⓐ Ⓑ Ⓒ Ⓓ
9 Ⓐ Ⓑ Ⓒ Ⓓ   12 Ⓕ Ⓖ Ⓗ Ⓙ   15 Ⓐ Ⓑ Ⓒ Ⓓ   18 Ⓕ Ⓖ Ⓗ Ⓙ

Answers: 7 C; 8 H; 9 B; 10 J; 11 B; 12 H; 13 A; 14 J; 15 C; 16 G; 17 B; 18 H

For numbers 19–24, darken the circle for the sentence that best combines the two sentences.

19 We waited twenty minutes.
The school bus finally came.
 A In twenty minutes we waited, and the school bus finally came.
 B We waited twenty minutes until the school bus finally came.
 C We and the school bus finally waited twenty minutes.
 D The school bus finally waited twenty minutes for us to come.

20 A path leads up to the house.
The Jefford family is building the house.
 F The house that the Jefford family is building is led up to by a path.
 G The Jefford family is building a house and a path.
 H A path leads up to the house that the Jefford family is building.
 J The Jefford family is building a house on the path that leads up to it.

21 The cat made a terrible racket last night.
The cat lives next door.
 A Last night's cat made a terrible racket next door.
 B A cat lives next door to the racket it made last night.
 C A cat made a terrible racket because it lives next door last night.
 D The cat that lives next door made a terrible racket last night.

22 The coach was upset.
No one showed up for practice.
 F No one, including the upset coach, showed up for practice.
 G The coach was upset because no one showed up for practice.
 H The practice that no one showed up for also made the coach upset.
 J The coach showed up for practice, and no one was upset.

23 Nadine enjoys team sports.
Nadine enjoys individual sports.
 A Nadine enjoys team sports and individual sports.
 B Nadine, an individual sport, enjoys team sports.
 C Nadine, who enjoys team sports, she also enjoys individual sports.
 D Nadine enjoys team sports because she enjoys individual sports.

24 We saw the old fire engine.
The old fire engine always leads the parade.
 F We lead the parade and saw the old fire engine.
 G We who saw the old fire engine led the parade.
 H We saw the old fire engine that always leads the parade.
 J Leading the parade, we saw the old fire engine.

19 Ⓐ Ⓑ Ⓒ Ⓓ   21 Ⓐ Ⓑ Ⓒ Ⓓ   23 Ⓐ Ⓑ Ⓒ Ⓓ
20 Ⓕ Ⓖ Ⓗ Ⓙ   22 Ⓕ Ⓖ Ⓗ Ⓙ   24 Ⓕ Ⓖ Ⓗ Ⓙ

Answers: 19 B; **20** D; **21** H; **22** G; **23** A; **24** H

For numbers 25–28, darken the circle for the topic sentence that best fits each paragraph.

25 _____. A mature polar bear weighs more than 1,500 pounds. Its coat, which appears white, offers excellent camouflage. Its dense mat of hairs also protects the bear from the severe cold. Underneath the coat is five inches of blubber for even more protection. The bear's feet are partially webbed to help it swim well. Its feet have hair on the soles. The hair keeps the bear from slipping on ice.

  A Grizzly bears are big bears, too.
  B Polar bears live in the Arctic.
  C Polar bears are fine hunters.
  D Polar bears are well suited for living in the Arctic.

26 _____. In the beginning scientists believed that dinosaurs were cold-blooded like crocodiles, lizards, and other modern reptiles. Then scientists wondered where dinosaurs got their energy to hunt. Cold-blooded animals slow down when the air grows cold. Scientists started to think that dinosaurs were warm-blooded. Now scientists are studying dinosaur bones again. In important ways dinosaurs have more in common with modern reptiles than with warm-blooded animals. Soon, scientists may again agree that dinosaurs were cold-blooded.

  F Many museums have dinosaur bones on display.
  G Were the dinosaurs warm-blooded or cold-blooded?
  H Are alligators and dinosaurs reptiles?
  J Scientists never know what to think.

27 _____. Telephones let us send voice messages. Fax machines let us send pictures. Modems let us send computer data. TV transmitters let us send pictures, sound, and movement. Radio and TV signals and telephone calls move at the speed of light to connect people, business, and government. We can talk from house to house, from city to city, and from continent to continent. Distance is not a barrier.

  A Maybe people have nothing to say to one another.
  B Many devices let people communicate quickly over long distances.
  C Telephones are sometimes a nuisance.
  D Telephone answering machines are terrific.

28 _____. There's a new ice cream store and two new restaurants. A skate store will open next month. It's taking the place of the toy store that closed. The old shoemaker's shop on the corner now sells vegetables. My mother says we need a meat store and a fish store. Our neighborhood is a real city neighborhood. It's always changing.

  F Some neighborhoods never change.
  G I like to window-shop with my friends.
  H Malls are fun to visit, too.
  J Stores are always opening and closing in this neighborhood.

GO ON

25 Ⓐ Ⓑ Ⓒ Ⓓ   27 Ⓐ Ⓑ Ⓒ Ⓓ
26 Ⓕ Ⓖ Ⓗ Ⓙ   28 Ⓕ Ⓖ Ⓗ Ⓙ

Answers: 25 D; 26 G; 27 B; 28 J

For numbers 29–32, darken the circle for the choice that gives the best supporting details to develop the topic sentence.

29 Tigers are the largest members of the cat family.
  A Siberian tigers live where the weather is very cold.
  B Mountain lions are known by many different names. Some people call this cat a puma, a cougar, a panther, or a catamount. By any name it is dangerous.
  C An adult male tiger often weighs more than four hundred pounds. Its body can be over nine feet long. Its tail alone is three feet long.
  D Siberian tigers live where the weather is very cold. They are related to the Indian tiger.

30 Dolphins are very intelligent animals.
  F Dolphins are speedy swimmers. Sometimes when they follow ships, they leap and jump high into the air.
  G They can communicate with one another underwater. They use clicks, barks, and whistles.
  H Like whales, dolphins are mammals. They use lungs to breathe.
  J Many sailors think that dolphins bring good luck. They say that a dolphin will save you from drowning.

31 Different birds eat different foods.
  A One reason birds can fly is that they have thin, hollow bones.
  B Most birds molt once a year. When they molt, they shed their old feathers and grow new ones.
  C Woodpeckers and hawks are blind and helpless when they are born. They must stay in their nests until they can open their eyes.
  D Sparrows like seeds. Shorebirds such as kingfishers and herons catch fish.

32 The two knobs on a giraffe's head are not true horns.
  F True horns, like the ones on cows, goats, and antelope grow throughout the animal's lifetime.
  G Bighorn sheep have feet that are especially good for climbing. They can pinch a rock between their toes.
  H Giraffes live in the grasslands of Africa. They have long tongues. They use these tongues to pluck leaves from trees.
  J A giraffe's coat has spots in it. These spots help camouflage the animal when it stands under a tree.

29 Ⓐ Ⓑ Ⓒ Ⓓ   31 Ⓐ Ⓑ Ⓒ Ⓓ
30 Ⓕ Ⓖ Ⓗ Ⓙ   32 Ⓕ Ⓖ Ⓗ Ⓙ

Answers: 29 C; 30 G; 31 D; 32 F

55

For numbers 33–36, darken the circle for the sentence that does <u>not</u> belong in the paragraph.

33 ¹Fireflies, or lightning bugs, are members of the beetle family. ²Ladybugs are beetles, too. ³Fireflies get their name from the cold light they emit from their abdomens. ⁴The light flashes on and off in patterns to attract other fireflies.

A sentence 1   **C** sentence 3
B sentence 2   **D** sentence 4

34 ¹There are many fancy breeds of cats, and then there's the domestic shorthair. ²Likewise, there are lots of breeds of dogs. ³Domestic shorthairs are the most common kind of cat in the United States. ⁴Now they're pets, but they used to be used to catch mice and rats.

F sentence 1   **H** sentence 3
G sentence 2   **J** sentence 4

35 ¹A jackrabbit isn't a rabbit at all. ²Jackrabbits are really hares. ³Isn't hare a strange name for an animal? ⁴Hares and rabbits are alike in many ways, but there are also some important differences.

A sentence 1   **C** sentence 3
B sentence 2   **D** sentence 4

36 ¹Some dogs are important work dogs. ²Collies are used to herd and protect sheep. ³German shepherds are excellent guard dogs. ⁴I want to enter my dog in the dog show someday .

F sentence 1   **H** sentence 3
G sentence 2   **J** sentence 4

33 Ⓐ Ⓑ Ⓒ Ⓓ   35 Ⓐ Ⓑ Ⓒ Ⓓ
34 Ⓕ Ⓖ Ⓗ Ⓙ   36 Ⓕ Ⓖ Ⓗ Ⓙ

Answers: 33 B; 34 G; 35 C; 36 J

For numbers 37–40, darken the circle for the sentence that best completes the paragraph.

37   There are three simple ways to tell moths and butterflies apart. If you see it during the day, it's probably a butterfly. At night, it's probably a moth. The antennae on a moth's head look like fat feathers. A butterfly's antennae look like thin rods. A moth spreads its wings flat when it lands. A butterfly holds its wings up. _____.

   A Moths can sometimes eat holes in wool clothing.
   B Monarch butterflies migrate south every fall.
   C Look closely—you may spot even more differences between moths and butterflies.
   D Moths and butterflies are insects.

38   Dalmatians are often shown as firehouse mascots. Dalmatians were originally hunting dogs. When the breed was introduced in England, they were trained as carriage dogs. They ran alongside the carriage and kept the driver company. In the United States they ran alongside the firefighters in their horse-drawn engines, unafraid of the fast-moving wheels. _____.

   F Other dogs were used as hunters.
   G Dalmatians are not born with spots.
   H Dalmatians also star in movies.
   J This is how Dalmatians became known as fire dogs.

39   Crickets are small, jumping, chirping insects. Crickets mostly chirp at night. But you've probably heard their cheerful music during the day if you've walked near an overgrown field. Crickets make their music by rubbing a rough part of one wing over a thick part of the other wing. _____.

   A Cricket is also the name of a sport.
   B Only female mosquitoes bite.
   C Crickets eat grass and other plants.
   D Some people think that crickets bring good luck.

40   Colts are young male horses. Young female horses are called fillies. Owners begin to train the young colts and fillies when they are a year old. The horse must be trained to wear a saddle and carry a rider. It must be trained to obey the rider's commands and signals. _____.

   F There are two styles of saddle—the western saddle and the English saddle.
   G The life span of a horse is twenty to thirty years.
   H Horse and rider must learn to work as a team.
   J Horses eat grass.

STOP

37 Ⓐ Ⓑ Ⓒ Ⓓ   39 Ⓐ Ⓑ Ⓒ Ⓓ
38 Ⓕ Ⓖ Ⓗ Ⓙ   40 Ⓕ Ⓖ Ⓗ Ⓙ

Answers: 37 C; 38 J; 39 D; 40 H

57

Test 6

Mathematical Computation

The Math Computation questions test how well you add, subtract, multiply, and divide. In this part of *TestWise*, you'll practice test-taking strategies you've been working on since the beginning. You will also learn some new strategies to help you handle questions about math.

Learn About the Strategies

Adjust to Changes in Format

The number of answer choices in this part changes from what you've gotten used to in earlier parts. In this part, each question is followed by four answer choices and a fifth choice, None of these. Remember to look at the letter of the answer choice you pick. Darken the correct one.

Make Sure You Know What Each Question Asks For

Look carefully at each question. Tell yourself whether you need to add, subtract, multiply, or divide. Don't misread signs and other directions. In this part, more than in other parts, answer choices will include likely mistakes you could make. For example,

Notice the sign!

$9 - 3 =$

A	3	Correct if you *divide* 9 by 3
B	12	Correct if you *add* 9 and 3
C	6	Correct if you *subtract* 3 from 9
D	27	Correct if you *multiply* 3 by 9
E	None of these	

Remember What You Know

When you come to a new problem, remember what you know. For instance, if you're adding decimals, remember that 2 and 2.0 are the same number. Remember that 1.9 is larger than 1.888 and smaller than 2. Remember to line up the decimal points when you add or subtract two decimals. When you multiply decimals, remember to count the correct number of decimal places in the product.

Check Your Answer

There's one *TestWise* strategy you've used from the beginning. That strategy is to think of your own answer first. Then find your answer in the choices. When you're answering math questions it's easy to make careless mistakes. Thus, you need a two-part strategy: Solve the problem. Then check your answer. Use adding to check your subtracting. Use multiplying to check your dividing. Use estimation skills, too.

What if I want to pick None of these? The *None of these* choice can be a trap. Do the problem again. Find out if you get the same answer twice.

Know Where *You* Make Mistakes

Are decimals your weak point? Do you have a hard time finding common denominators when you work with fractions? Do you forget how to multiply fractions?

Remember where you are likely to make mistakes. When you get to a kind of problem that causes you difficulties, take a deep breath. Then slow down. Do this problem carefully.

19. Adding

Directions: Darken the circle for the correct answer. Darken the circle for <u>None of these</u> if the answer is <u>not</u> given.

Sample A

$64 + 8.542 =$

A 8.806
B 55.458
C 72.542
D 546.688
E None of these

> Remember what you know—64.000 is another way to write 64.

STOP

> I'll find my own answer to the problem before I check the choices.

1 $\frac{3}{8} + \frac{1}{2} + \frac{1}{4} =$

A $\frac{3}{4}$
B 1
C $1\frac{1}{8}$
D $1\frac{3}{8}$
E None of these

2 $\begin{array}{r} 2.7 \\ + 2.55 \end{array}$

F 282
G 5.25
H 2.82
J 5.15
K None of these

3 $\frac{6}{10} + \frac{23}{100} =$

A $\frac{29}{100}$
B $\frac{73}{10}$
C $\frac{138}{100}$
D $\frac{83}{100}$
E None of these

4 $44 + 57 + 63 =$

F 164
G 174
H 163
J 107.3
K None of these

5 $\frac{1}{11} + \frac{10}{11} =$

A $1\frac{1}{11}$
B 11
C $\frac{11}{22}$
D 1
E None of these

6 $\begin{array}{r} 7567 \\ 6649 \\ + 9871 \end{array}$

F 23,087
G 23,086
H 24.087
J 24,087
K None of these

7 $\frac{1}{6} + \frac{1}{3} =$

A $\frac{2}{9}$
B $\frac{2}{6}$
C $\frac{2}{3}$
D $\frac{1}{2}$
E None of these

8 $42 + 7.665 =$

F 7.707
G 49.665
H 49.17
J 50.0
K None of these

> If I change my answer, I have to erase the old answer completely.

STOP

A Ⓐ Ⓑ Ⓒ Ⓓ Ⓔ   2 Ⓕ Ⓖ Ⓗ Ⓙ Ⓚ   4 Ⓕ Ⓖ Ⓗ Ⓙ Ⓚ   6 Ⓕ Ⓖ Ⓗ Ⓙ Ⓚ   8 Ⓕ Ⓖ Ⓗ Ⓙ Ⓚ
1 Ⓐ Ⓑ Ⓒ Ⓓ Ⓔ   3 Ⓐ Ⓑ Ⓒ Ⓓ Ⓔ   5 Ⓐ Ⓑ Ⓒ Ⓓ Ⓔ   7 Ⓐ Ⓑ Ⓒ Ⓓ Ⓔ

Answers: A C; 1 C; 2 G; 3 D; 4 F; 5 D; 6 J; 7 D; 8 G

20. Subtracting

Directions: Darken the circle for the correct answer. Darken the circle for <u>None of these</u> if the answer is <u>not</u> given.

Sample A

$\frac{7}{8} - \frac{3}{8} =$

A 1¼
B ⁷⁄₁₆
C ⅝
D ½
E None of these

> I won't get confused. All the questions on this page are subtraction questions.

> I need to remember to check my answers by adding.

1

$604 - 595 =$

A 8
B 9
C 19
D 10
E None of these

2

6443
− 2770

F 3683
G 3773
H 3763
J 3673
K None of these

3

5000
− 3689

A 311
B 1311
C 2311
D 1312
E None of these

4

9.5
− 2.65

F 6.85
G 6.05
H 7.05
J 7.6
K None of these

5

$\$25.45 - \$4.95 =$

A $21.05
B $19.95
C $20.50
D $20.05
E None of these

6

$4 - 3.69 =$

F 4.9
G .69
H 1.31
J .31
K None of these

7

$\$49.95 - \$3.97 =$

A 45.2
B 45.98
C 45.02
D 46.02
E None of these

8

$\frac{7}{8} - \frac{1}{8} =$

F ¼
G ¾
H ⅝
J ⅔
K None of these

> I'll make sure not to darken a circle next to the wrong number.

A (A)(B)(C)(D)(E)   2 (F)(G)(H)(J)(K)   4 (F)(G)(H)(J)(K)   6 (F)(G)(H)(J)(K)   8 (F)(G)(H)(J)(K)
1 (A)(B)(C)(D)(E)   3 (A)(B)(C)(D)(E)   5 (A)(B)(C)(D)(E)   7 (A)(B)(C)(D)(E)

Answers: A D; 1 B; 2 J; 3 B; 4 F; 5 C; 6 J; 7 B; 8 G

21. Multiplying

Directions: Darken the circle for the correct answer. Darken the circle for <u>None of these</u> if the answer is <u>not</u> given.

Sample A

75 X 74 =

A 4,550
B 5,550
C 4,650
D 4,560
E None of these

I need to watch out for decimal points.

STOP

I'll read the answer choices carefully. I don't want to pick the wrong answer by mistake.

1

35 X 25 =

A 875
B 870
C 8,700
D 6,165
E None of these

2

79 x 19 =

F 1,600
G 790
H 8,611
J 1,501
K None of these

3

6.1 X 6 =

A 36.6
B 3.66
C 366
D 6.7
E None of these

4

59.5 X 6.79 =

F 4040.05
G 404.005
H 40400.5
J 580.72
K None of these

5

½ X ¼ =

A ¼
B ¹⁄₁₆
C ⅓
D ⅛
E None of these

6

½
x 8

F ¹⁄₁₆
G 16
H 4
J ¼
K None of these

7

0.05
x 5

A 0.25
B 0.025
C 25
D 2.5
E None of these

8

93 x 37 =

F 28,551
G 930
H 3,563
J 2,331
K None of these

Did I darken the right circle?

STOP

A Ⓐ Ⓑ Ⓒ Ⓓ Ⓔ   2 Ⓕ Ⓖ Ⓗ Ⓙ Ⓚ   4 Ⓕ Ⓖ Ⓗ Ⓙ Ⓚ   6 Ⓕ Ⓖ Ⓗ Ⓙ Ⓚ   8 Ⓕ Ⓖ Ⓗ Ⓙ Ⓚ
1 Ⓐ Ⓑ Ⓒ Ⓓ Ⓔ   3 Ⓐ Ⓑ Ⓒ Ⓓ Ⓔ   5 Ⓐ Ⓑ Ⓒ Ⓓ Ⓔ   7 Ⓐ Ⓑ Ⓒ Ⓓ Ⓔ

Answers: A B; 1 A; 2 J; 3 A; 4 G; 5 D; 6 H; 7 A; 8 K

22. Dividing

Directions: Darken the circle for the correct answer. Darken the circle for <u>None of these</u> if the answer is <u>not</u> given.

Sample A

$$64 \div 64 =$$

    A   0
    B   1
    C   .5
    D   .1
    E   None of these

I'll do each problem myself *before* I check the answer choices.

STOP

Let me take my time on problems I find difficult.

1

$7\overline{)49}$

    A   7
    B   8
    C   6
    D   6.5
    E   None of these

2

$24\overline{)720}$

    F   4
    G   30
    H   3
    J   25
    K   None of these

3

$16\overline{)1216}$

    A   76
    B   34
    C   67
    D   13
    E   None of these

4

$$68 \div 10 =$$

    F   680
    G   .68
    H   .068
    J   6.8
    K   None of these

5

$$625 \div 25 =$$

    A   15
    B   25
    C   20
    D   31
    E   None of these

6

$$79 \div 10 =$$

    F   79
    G   7.9
    H   .79
    J   790
    K   None of these

7

$$800 \div 40 =$$

    A   4
    B   16
    C   20
    D   24
    E   None of these

8

$12\overline{)156}$

    F   10.3
    G   12
    H   12.3
    J   13
    K   None of these

STOP

Have I darkened a circle next to each number?

A   Ⓐ Ⓑ Ⓒ Ⓓ Ⓔ   2   Ⓕ Ⓖ Ⓗ Ⓙ Ⓚ   4   Ⓕ Ⓖ Ⓗ Ⓙ Ⓚ   6   Ⓕ Ⓖ Ⓗ Ⓙ Ⓚ   8   Ⓕ Ⓖ Ⓗ Ⓙ Ⓚ
1   Ⓐ Ⓑ Ⓒ Ⓓ Ⓔ   3   Ⓐ Ⓑ Ⓒ Ⓓ Ⓔ   5   Ⓐ Ⓑ Ⓒ Ⓓ Ⓔ   7   Ⓐ Ⓑ Ⓒ Ⓓ Ⓔ

Mathematical Computation

Suggested time: 30 minutes

Read aloud to the class:

The questions on each part of the Math Computation test are just like the questions you have been practicing.

Read the directions for each group of questions. Read the questions and the answer choices carefully. Then darken the circle for each correct answer. Keep working until you reach the word *STOP* at the bottom of page 66. Then put your pencil down.

For numbers 1–8, darken the circle for the correct answer. Darken the circle for <u>None of these</u> if the answer is <u>not</u> given.

1 $\frac{1}{3} + \frac{1}{3} + \frac{2}{3} =$

A $1\frac{2}{3}$
B $\frac{7}{8}$
C $\frac{2}{3}$
D $1\frac{1}{3}$
E None of these

5 $\frac{1}{9} + \frac{7}{9} =$

A 1
B $\frac{8}{99}$
C $\frac{8}{9}$
D $\frac{8}{18}$
E None of these

2
3.4
+ 6.59

F 9.99
G 9.63
H 6.93
J 40.59
K None of these

6
2001
7732
+ 8989

F 17,723
G 18,722
H 18,723
J 18,622
K None of these

3 $\frac{3}{10} + \frac{45}{100} =$

A 48/100
B 48/110
C 42/100
D $\frac{3}{4}$
E None of these

7 $\frac{5}{8} + \frac{7}{8} =$

A $\frac{12}{16}$
B $\frac{3}{4}$
C $1\frac{1}{8}$
D $1\frac{1}{2}$
E None of these

4 $66 + 75 + 4 =$

F 144
G 141
H 146
J 149
K None of these

8 $36 + 459.2 =$

F 495.2
G 49.52
H 4,952
J 459.38
K None of these

GO ON ➡

1 Ⓐ Ⓑ Ⓒ Ⓓ Ⓔ   3 Ⓐ Ⓑ Ⓒ Ⓓ Ⓔ   5 Ⓐ Ⓑ Ⓒ Ⓓ Ⓔ   7 Ⓐ Ⓑ Ⓒ Ⓓ Ⓔ
2 Ⓕ Ⓖ Ⓗ Ⓙ Ⓚ   4 Ⓕ Ⓖ Ⓗ Ⓙ Ⓚ   6 Ⓕ Ⓖ Ⓗ Ⓙ Ⓚ   8 Ⓕ Ⓖ Ⓗ Ⓙ Ⓚ

Answers: 1 D; **2** F; **3** D; **4** K; **5** C; **6** G; **7** D; **8** F

For numbers 9–18, darken the circle for the correct answer. Darken the circle for <u>None of these</u> if the answer is <u>not</u> given.

9

$$324 - 179 =$$

- **A** 143
- **B** 144
- **C** 245
- **D** 145
- **E** None of these

10

$$7 - 6.03 =$$

- **F** 1.97
- **G** .097
- **H** .97
- **J** .79
- **K** None of these

11

$$7.23 \\ -\ 3.03$$

- **A** 3.19
- **B** 4.2
- **C** 3.2
- **D** 42
- **E** None of these

12

$$\tfrac{3}{4} - \tfrac{1}{2} =$$

- **F** 0
- **G** ⅛
- **H** ½
- **J** ¼
- **K** None of these

13

$$\$65.01 - \$54.79 =$$

- **A** $10.80
- **B** $10.78
- **C** $11.78
- **D** $10.22
- **E** None of these

14

$$\$16.98 - \$2.02 =$$

- **F** $14.78
- **G** $14.96
- **H** $14.00
- **J** $16.00
- **K** None of these

15

$$6723 \\ -\ 2199$$

- **A** 4,524
- **B** 4,514
- **C** 4,522
- **D** 4,526
- **E** None of these

16

$$98.7 - 64.8 =$$

- **F** 33.1
- **G** 33.9
- **H** 3.39
- **J** 34.5
- **K** None of these

17

$$12.4 \\ -\ 6.56$$

- **A** 5.84
- **B** 5.48
- **C** 5.80
- **D** 6.52
- **E** None of these

18

$$\tfrac{7}{8} - \tfrac{3}{8} =$$

- **F** ½
- **G** ⅛
- **H** 1⁄16
- **J** ¼
- **K** None of these

9 Ⓐ Ⓑ Ⓒ Ⓓ Ⓔ 11 Ⓐ Ⓑ Ⓒ Ⓓ Ⓔ 13 Ⓐ Ⓑ Ⓒ Ⓓ Ⓔ 15 Ⓐ Ⓑ Ⓒ Ⓓ Ⓔ 17 Ⓐ Ⓑ Ⓒ Ⓓ Ⓔ
10 Ⓕ Ⓖ Ⓗ Ⓙ Ⓚ 12 Ⓕ Ⓖ Ⓗ Ⓙ Ⓚ 14 Ⓕ Ⓖ Ⓗ Ⓙ Ⓚ 16 Ⓕ Ⓖ Ⓗ Ⓙ Ⓚ 18 Ⓕ Ⓖ Ⓗ Ⓙ Ⓚ

Answers: 9 D; 10 H; 11 B; 12 J; 13 D; 14 G; 15 A; 16 G; 17 A; 18 F

For numbers 19–28, darken the circle for the correct answer. Darken the circle for <u>None of these</u> if the answer is <u>not</u> given.

19

15 x 15 =

A 25
B 22.5
C 225
D 2225
E None of these

20

1.9 x .5 =

F .95
G 9.5
H .095
J 46
K None of these

21

450 x 25 =

A 31,500
B 1,125
C 11,250
D 3,150
E None of these

22

.55 x .55 =

F .3025
G .03025
H 3.025
J 30.25
K None of these

23

⅓
x 9

A ½₇
B 3
C 6
D ⅓
E None of these

24

145 x 366 =

F 5,307.0
G 2,175
H 53,070
J 6,090
K None of these

25

7.7 x .04 =

A .308
B .0308
C 30.8
D 308
E None of these

26

98.7 – 64.8 =

F 33.1
G 34.5
H 3.39
J 33.9
K None of these

27

89
x 12

A 1800
B 980
C 168
D 267
E None of these

28

.75 x 100 =

F 1.75
G .75
H 75
J 750
K None of these

19 Ⓐ Ⓑ Ⓒ Ⓓ Ⓔ   21 Ⓐ Ⓑ Ⓒ Ⓓ Ⓔ   23 Ⓐ Ⓑ Ⓒ Ⓓ Ⓔ   25 Ⓐ Ⓑ Ⓒ Ⓓ Ⓔ   27 Ⓐ Ⓑ Ⓒ Ⓓ Ⓔ
20 Ⓕ Ⓖ Ⓗ Ⓙ Ⓚ   22 Ⓕ Ⓖ Ⓗ Ⓙ Ⓚ   24 Ⓕ Ⓖ Ⓗ Ⓙ Ⓚ   26 Ⓕ Ⓖ Ⓗ Ⓙ Ⓚ   28 Ⓕ Ⓖ Ⓗ Ⓙ Ⓚ

Answers: 19 C; **20** C; **21** F; **22** F; **23** B; **24** H; **25** A; **26** J; **27** E; **28** H

For numbers 29–38, darken the circle for the correct answer. Darken the circle for <u>None of these</u> if the answer is <u>not</u> given.

29

$270 \div 3 =$

A 9
B 90
C 99
D 9.1
E None of these

30

$1.9 \times .5 =$

F .995
G 9.95
H .095
J .95
K None of these

31

$7 \overline{)4949}$

A 707
B 77
C 7007
D 770
E None of these

32

$27 \div 10 =$

F 270
G 27
H .027
J 2.7
K None of these

33

$960 \div 8 =$

A 14
B 90
C 120
D 12
E None of these

34

$5 \overline{)26}$

F 3
G 4
H 5
J 6
K None of these

35

$3 \overline{)369}$

A 12
B 23
C 132
D 123
E None of these

36

$40 \div .5 =$

F 80
G 200
H 20
J 8
K None of these

37

$450 \div 15 =$

A 3
B 5
C 30
D 33
E None of these

38

$7 \overline{)56}$

F 7
G 8
H 6
J 5
K None of these

STOP

29 Ⓐ Ⓑ Ⓒ Ⓓ Ⓔ   31 Ⓐ Ⓑ Ⓒ Ⓓ Ⓔ   33 Ⓐ Ⓑ Ⓒ Ⓓ Ⓔ   35 Ⓐ Ⓑ Ⓒ Ⓓ Ⓔ   37 Ⓐ Ⓑ Ⓒ Ⓓ Ⓔ
30 Ⓕ Ⓖ Ⓗ Ⓙ Ⓚ   32 Ⓕ Ⓖ Ⓗ Ⓙ Ⓚ   34 Ⓕ Ⓖ Ⓗ Ⓙ Ⓚ   36 Ⓕ Ⓖ Ⓗ Ⓙ Ⓚ   38 Ⓕ Ⓖ Ⓗ Ⓙ Ⓚ

Answers: 29 B; 30 J; 31 A; 32 J; 33 C; 34 K; 35 D; 36 F; 37 C; 38 G

Mathematical Concepts and Applications

The Math Concepts and Applications questions test how well you can use math to solve problems. In this part of TestWise, you'll practice the time strategies and answer-sheet strategies you've been working on since the beginning. You will also learn some new strategies to help you handle questions about mathematics.

Learn About the Strategies

Make Sure You Know What the Problem Asks You to Do

On a test you have to know what to do before you can do it. Directions are always important. In this part of the test, each math problem is different. Each problem gives you a new set of directions. Each time you start a new problem, you need to tell yourself in your own words what the problem is about. Here are some questions to ask yourself:

- What is the problem about?
- How is the information related?
- Have I ever solved a problem like this one before? What did I do?
- What clues tell me what the answer should show?
- What clues tell me to add, subtract, multiply, or divide?

Don't Get Bogged Down

Some problems may take longer than others to solve. Skip problems that may take too much time. Come back to them later. *Caution:* When you skip a problem, make sure to leave its answer space blank, too.

Get the Arithmetic Right

Don't miss the answer because you added 6 and 5 and got 10. Check your answer *before* you look at the answer choices. First be sure you picked the right numbers to work with. Then add, subtract, multiply, or divide the numbers again. Be sure your two answers agree.

Read Charts and Diagrams with Care

Some of the problems in this test may ask you about charts and diagrams. Study charts and diagrams carefully. Make sure you know what they show and why they're included.

Remember What You Know

When you come to a new problem, think about it. Remember what you know. Are you measuring? Comparing? Working with triangles or other figures? Be cool-headed. Think about similar problems you've solved successfully.

Don't waste time trying to solve a kind of problem you've never seen before. Skip it. Come back to it at the end.

23. Understanding Numeration

Directions: Darken the circle for the correct answer to each question.

Sample A

Which decimal equals ¾?

A .25
B .3
C .5
D .75

What do i know about decimals? If this were dollars, how much is three-fourths of a dollar?

STOP

What is each problem asking for?

1 If you estimate the answer to 19.2 + 223 by rounding to the nearest ten, which numbers should you use?

A 20 + 220
B 20 +230
C 19 + 225
D 10 + 230

2 Which fraction is closest to 1?

F ⅓
G ½
H ⅝
J ⅞

3 Which number sentence would you use to find the number missing from the pattern?

10, 20, 40, 80, ____, 320

A 10 + 20 + 40 + 80 = 150
B 40 + 80 = 120
C 80 x 2 = 160
D 320 - 80 = 240

4 Which of these means the same as 15.2 million?

F 15,000,002
G 15,000,200
H 15,002,000
J 15,200,000

5 Which is the greatest common factor of 10, 15, and 25?

A 3
B 4
C 5
D 10

6 What is the next number in this progression?

3, 5, 8, 12, 17, 23, ____

F 28
G 29
H 30
J 31

STOP

If I skip a question, I have to skip an answer number, too.

A Ⓐ Ⓑ Ⓒ Ⓓ   2 Ⓕ Ⓖ Ⓗ Ⓙ   4 Ⓕ Ⓖ Ⓗ Ⓙ   6 Ⓕ Ⓖ Ⓗ Ⓙ
1 Ⓐ Ⓑ Ⓒ Ⓓ   3 Ⓐ Ⓑ Ⓒ Ⓓ   5 Ⓐ Ⓑ Ⓒ Ⓓ

Answers: A D; 1 A; 2 J; 3 C; 4 J; 5 C; 6 H

24. Solving Problems

Directions: Darken the circle for the correct answer to each question.

Sample A

Each hockey team needs five players and a goalie. The new league has five teams. How many team members are needed in all.

A 5
B 25
C 30
D 35

"In all" gives me a clue. Should I add or multiply?

STOP

I'll read each problem carefully.

1 Tom is taller than Jonah. Danielle is taller than Tom. Dee is shorter than Jonah. Who is the shortest?
A Tom
B Jonah
C Danielle
D Dee

2 Parking lot one holds 400 cars. Parking lot two holds 100 fewer cars. How many cars can both parking lots hold together when both parking lots are full.
F 300
G 500
H 700
J 4000

3 Which number makes both number sentences correct?

$3 \times \square = 27$

$36 \div \square = 4$

A 6
B 8
C 9
D 12

4 Beth and Josh made five boxes of treats for their friends. Each box holds 20 treats, but Josh ate one treat from each box. How many treats are left?
F 5
G 19
H 95
J 105

5 On a weekday, 100 cars cross the bridge every hour from 8:00 AM to 8:00 PM. How many cars in all cross the bridge during those hours?
A 800
B 1,000
C 1,200
D 8,000

6 Kyra wanted to make 75 holiday decorations to sell at the craft fair. On Monday she made 25. On Tuesday she made 12. How many more must she make to reach her goal?
F 37
G 38
H 50
J 63

STOP

I'll darken every circle completely.

A Ⓐ Ⓑ Ⓒ Ⓓ   2 Ⓕ Ⓖ Ⓗ Ⓙ   4 Ⓕ Ⓖ Ⓗ Ⓙ   6 Ⓕ Ⓖ Ⓗ Ⓙ
1 Ⓐ Ⓑ Ⓒ Ⓓ   3 Ⓐ Ⓑ Ⓒ Ⓓ   5 Ⓐ Ⓑ Ⓒ Ⓓ

Answers: A C; 1 D; 2 H; 3 C; 4 H; 5 C; 6 G

I'll read all the questions.
Then I'll read the menu again.

Big Pizza Restaurant The Original and Still the Best!

Whole Pies	Small	Medium	Large	Other		Drinks	
Round Pizza	$5.00	$7.50	$10.00	Salad		Soft Drinks	$1.00
Square Pizza	6.00	9.50	12.00	Small	$3.00	Hot Chocolate	.75
Each Extra Topping	.50	.75	1.00	Large	4.50	Milk	.75
The Works	2.00	3.00	4.00	Bread Sticks (12)	2.00	Coffee, Tea	.75
				Assorted pastries			
				(each)	2.00		

Toppings
Extra Cheese, Mushroom,
Sausage, Hot Sausage,
Peppers, Anchovies,

By the Slice
Round Pizza $1.40
Square Pizza   1.60
Topping (each) .50

School Special—*Weekdays Only*
Slice of Round Pizza and Soft Drink $1.50

 I'll tell myself what each problem wants me to find out.

For questions 7–12, use the information in the box above.

7 Ivy ordered 1 medium square pizza with 3 extra toppings and 1 order of bread sticks. How much did she pay?
A $13.75
B $15.50
C $17.00
D $19.00

8 If Jess had to pay for each item in the School Special by itself, how much would he pay?
F $1.40
G $2.15
H $2.40
J $2.60

9 Mike ordered 1 small round pizza with no extra toppings and 1 small salad. How much did he pay?
A $7.50
B $8.00
C $8.50
D $9.50

10 Angela can spend up to $10.00. Which of the following will she be able to buy?
F   1 medium square pizza with 2 toppings
G   1 medium round pizza with 3 toppings
H   2 small round pizzas and 1 hot chocolate
J   1 medium round pizza and 1 large salad

11 Jane ordered 1 large square pie with two extra toppings, 3 pastries, and 3 soft drinks. How much did Jane pay?
A $18.00
B $20.00
C $23.00
D $25.00

12 Greg bought 1 slice of square pizza and 1 milk. He paid with a $5 bill. How much charge did he receive?
F $1.55
G $1.75
H $2.35
J $2.65

 STOP

I'll check to be sure my answers are in the right places.

7   Ⓐ Ⓑ Ⓒ Ⓓ   9   Ⓐ Ⓑ Ⓒ Ⓓ   11   Ⓐ Ⓑ Ⓒ Ⓓ
8   Ⓕ Ⓖ Ⓗ Ⓙ   10   Ⓕ Ⓖ Ⓗ Ⓙ   12   Ⓕ Ⓖ Ⓗ Ⓙ

 Answers: 7 A; 8 H; 9 B; 10 G; 11 C; 12 J

25. Tables, Charts, and Graphs

Directions: Darken the circle for the correct answer to each question.

Sample A

This graph shows the number of books read by the fifth grade classes last month.

Classes

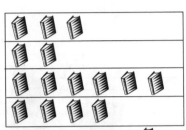

Class 5–1

Class 5–2

Class 5–3

Class 5–4

Number of books   Each = 10 books

Which class read more than 30 books but fewer than 60 books?

A Class 5–1
B Class 5–2
C Class 5–3
D Class 5–4

The scale at the bottom helps me understand the graph.

STOP

I'll read the questions first. They will tell me what to look for on the graph.

This graph shows the number of servings of breakfast foods that were sold by a cafeteria. Study the graph. Then answer questions 1–3.

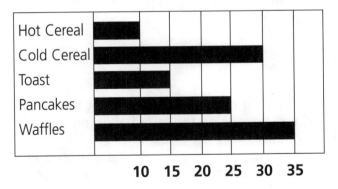

Hot Cereal
Cold Cereal
Toast
Pancakes
Waffles

10 15 20 25 30 35

1 Which was the most popular breakfast food?
A cold cereal
B toast
C waffles
D pancakes

2 How many servings of hot cereal and cold cereal were served?
F 15
G 25
H 35
J 40

3 If the people who ordered toast had ordered pancakes instead, which would be the most popular breakfast food?
A hot cereal
B cold cereal
C waffles
D pancakes

GO ON

I'll be sure to darken the right circle.

A Ⓐ Ⓑ Ⓒ Ⓓ   2 Ⓕ Ⓖ Ⓗ Ⓙ
1 Ⓐ Ⓑ Ⓒ Ⓓ   3 Ⓐ Ⓑ Ⓒ Ⓓ

Answers: A D; 1 C; 2 J; 3 D

I need to read each question carefully to find out what to do.

This table shows the number of students in a class who play specific sports. Study the table. Then answer questions 4 and 5.

Sport	Number of Players
Soccer	18
Baseball	8
Softball	6
Basketball	10
In-line Skating	20

4 How many more students play soccer than basketball?
   A 6
   B 8
   C 10
   D 12

5 If 5 students switch from baseball to soccer, how many soccer players will there be?
   F 18
   G 20
   H 23
   J 25

This pie chart shows which flavors of yogurt students in one class like. Study the pie chart. Then answer question 6.

6 Which is the least liked flavor of yogurt?
   A vanilla
   B chocolate
   C strawberry
   D plain

This graph shows the number of cups of lemonade sold each hour during the four hours that Mike and Marla's lemonade stand was open. Study the graph. Then answer questions 7–9.

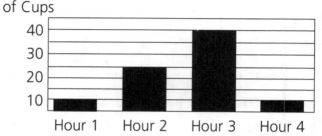

7 During which hour did Mike and Marla's lemonade stand get the most business?
   F hour 1
   G hour 2
   H hour 3
   J hour 4

8 How many cups of lemonade did Mike and Marla sell during all 4 hours?
   A 65
   B 75
   C 85
   D 95

9 Which of these questions <u>cannot</u> be answered using the information on the graph?
   F When did they sell the least lemonade?
   G When did they sell the most lemonade?
   H Which hours were the best hours to sell lemonade?
   J How much money did they make?

STOP

I won't lose my place. I'll mark the correct answer circles.

4 Ⓐ Ⓑ Ⓒ Ⓓ   6 Ⓐ Ⓑ Ⓒ Ⓓ   8 Ⓐ Ⓑ Ⓒ Ⓓ
5 Ⓕ Ⓖ Ⓗ Ⓙ   7 Ⓕ Ⓖ Ⓗ Ⓙ   9 Ⓕ Ⓖ Ⓗ Ⓙ

Answers: 4 B; 5 H; 6 D; 7 H; 8 C; 9 J

Practice the Strategies

26. Understanding Measurement and Geometry

Directions: Darken the circle for the correct answer to each question.

Sample A

What is the area of the rectangle shown?
(Area = length x width)

A 2 square feet
B 8 square feet
C 15 square feet
D 45 square feet

3 feet

5 feet

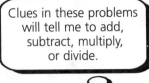
Clues in these problems will tell me to add, subtract, multiply, or divide.

STOP

Each problem is different. I need to read each one carefully.

1 Norma was sent to the store to buy a gallon of milk. No gallon containers were left. Which of the following containers of milk could she buy instead?

A 4 pints
B 6 pints
C 4 quarts
D 8 quarts

2 What is the length of the ruler from A to B?

F 3¼
G 3½
H 3¾
J 3⅞

3 Which of the following figures is a triangle?

A □
B ⬡
C △
D ⬠

4 What is the perimeter of the figure below?

F 10 feet
G 17 feet
H 18 feet
J 252 feet

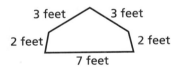
3 feet   3 feet
2 feet   2 feet
7 feet

GO ON

Did I darken only one circle next to each number?

A Ⓐ Ⓑ Ⓒ Ⓓ   2 Ⓕ Ⓖ Ⓗ Ⓙ   4 Ⓕ Ⓖ Ⓗ Ⓙ
1 Ⓐ Ⓑ Ⓒ Ⓓ   3 Ⓐ Ⓑ Ⓒ Ⓓ

© 1998 by Troll Communications L.L.C.

Answers: A C; 1 C; 2 G; 3 C; 4 G

73

I'll take my time and read each problem carefully.

5 What is the perimeter of the shaded portion of the figure below.

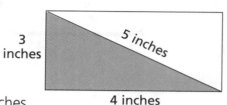

3 inches

5 inches

4 inches

A 5 inches
B 12 inches
C 19 inches
D 24 inches

6 An object that weighs 1 pound is placed on one side of a scale. Which of the following weights must be placed on the other side of the scale to make the scale balance?

F two 2-ounce weights
G two 6-ounce weights
H two 6-ounce weights and two 2-ounce weights.
J three 3-ounce weights

7 Which temperature would the thermometer show if the temperature rose 7 degrees?

A 25 degrees
B 30 degrees
C 32 degrees
D 35 degrees

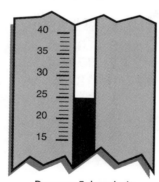

Degrees Fahrenheit

8 What is the area of the rectangle shown? (Area = length x width)

3 feet

6 feet

F 6 square feet
G 9 square feet
H 12 square feet
J 18 square feet

9 What is the length of the ruler from A to B?
A 5 meters
B 5 millimeters
C 5 centimeters
D 6 centimeters

10 What is the total number of squares on a checkerboard if each side is divided into 8 squares?
F 16
G 32
H 64
J 128

GO ON

Let me make sure I get the numbers right. This page starts with question 5.

5 Ⓐ Ⓑ Ⓒ Ⓓ   7 Ⓐ Ⓑ Ⓒ Ⓓ   9 Ⓐ Ⓑ Ⓒ Ⓓ
6 Ⓕ Ⓖ Ⓗ Ⓙ   8 Ⓕ Ⓖ Ⓗ Ⓙ   10 Ⓕ Ⓖ Ⓗ Ⓙ

Answers: 5 B; 6 H; 7 C; 8 J; 9 C; 10 H

27. Fractions and Money

Directions: Darken the circle for the correct answer to each question.

Sample A

Which of the following is equal to $2.45?

A 2 dollar bills, 2 quarters, 1 nickel
B 1 dollar bill, 5 quarters, 2 dimes
C 1 dollar bill, 6 quarters, 1 dime
D 2 dollar bills, 3 dimes, 5 nickels

I must make sure I get the arithmetic right. I'll check my answers.

STOP

I'll find my own answer before I look at the answer choices.

1 Which fraction tells how many circles in the group are darkened?

A ½
B ⅔
C ¾
D ⅞

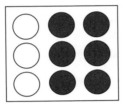

2 Molly wants to buy a package of modeling clay. The clay sells for $2.79. She has a $1 bill and 3 quarters with her. How much more money does she need?

F $0.04
G $0.40
H $1.04
J $1.40

3 Anne has 4 quarters and 5 dimes. Brenda has 2 dollar bills and 2 nickels. What is the most they could spend together to buy a gift?

A $2.75
B $3.50
C $3.60
D $4.00

4 The pizza pie was divided into 8 slices. Beth and Judy each ate 1 slice. Which fraction expresses how much of the pizza is left?

F ⅔
G ⅝
H ⅞
J ¾

5 Mark needs to buy a package of party balloons. Mark has $1.50 in his pocket. The balloons are marked $4.29. How much more money does he need?

A $1.71
B $2.71
C $2.79
D $3.79

6 Which of these boxes has ⅓ of the circles darkened?

F

G

H

J

GO ON

I'll erase completely every answer I change.

A Ⓐ Ⓑ Ⓒ Ⓓ   2 Ⓕ Ⓖ Ⓗ Ⓙ   4 Ⓕ Ⓖ Ⓗ Ⓙ   6 Ⓕ Ⓖ Ⓗ Ⓙ
1 Ⓐ Ⓑ Ⓒ Ⓓ   3 Ⓐ Ⓑ Ⓒ Ⓓ   5 Ⓐ Ⓑ Ⓒ Ⓓ

Answers: A B; 1 B; 2 H; 3 C; 4 J; 5 C; 6 G

Mathematical Concepts and Applications

Suggested time: 50 minutes

Read aloud to the class:

The questions on each part of the Math Concepts and Applications test are just like the questions you have been practicing.

Read the directions for each group of questions. Read the questions and the answer choices carefully. Then darken the circle for each correct answer. Keep working until you reach the word *STOP* at the bottom of page 83. Then put your pencil down.

For numbers 1–6, darken the circle for the correct answer to each question.

1 Which number sentence would you use to find the next number in this pattern?

2, 4, 8, 16, 32, 64, ____

A 32 + 64 = 96
B 2 + 4 + 8 + 16 + 32 + 64 = 126
C 2 x 64 = 128
D 3 x 64 = 192

2 Which is the greatest common factor of 9, 27, and 36?
F 1
G 3
H 6
J 9

3 What is the next number in this progression?

3, 6, 9, 4, 8, 12, 5, 10, 15, ____

A 6
B 18
C 20
D 30

4 Which group of numbers is in order from greatest to least?
F 75, 74, 64, 4, 14
G 4, 8, 12, 16, 20
H 8, 6, 3, 2, 1, .5
J 4.5, 5, 4, 3, 2, 1

5 Which of these fractions means the same as .2?
A ½
B ⅓
C ¼
D ⅕

6 If you estimate the answer to 52 x 98 by rounding to the nearest ten, which numbers should you use?
F 50 X 100
G 55 X 100
H 50 X 95
J 55 X 95

GO ON

---

1 Ⓐ Ⓑ Ⓒ Ⓓ   3 Ⓐ Ⓑ Ⓒ Ⓓ   5 Ⓐ Ⓑ Ⓒ Ⓓ
2 Ⓕ Ⓖ Ⓗ Ⓙ   4 Ⓕ Ⓖ Ⓗ Ⓙ   6 Ⓕ Ⓖ Ⓗ Ⓙ

Answers: 1 C; 2 J; 3 A; 4 H; 5 D; 6 F

For numbers 7–20, darken the circle for the correct answer to each question.

7 Which number makes both number sentences correct?

$$6 \times \square = 48$$
$$64 \div \square = 8$$

A 6
B 7
C 8
D 9

8 Denise is older than Terri. Vera is older than Denise. Joan is younger than Terri. Who is the oldest?

F Denise
G Terri
H Vera
J Joan

9 Closet one holds 35 coats. Closet two holds 7 more coats than closet one. How many coats can both closets hold when both closets are full?

A 42
B 63
C 70
D 77

10 Which number makes both number sentences correct?

$$5 \times \square = 55$$
$$44 \div \square = 4$$

F 5
G 7
H 9
J 11

11 Dave wanted to score 16 goals in 6 games. In the first four games, he scored 2 goals in each game. In the fifth game he scored 4 goals. How many goals must he score in the sixth game in order to score 16 goals in all?

A 3
B 4
C 5
D 6

12 Everyone in the group needs two pencils. Anne sharpened 15 red pencils and 20 blue pencils. How many black pencils must she sharpen so that everyone in the group can have one black pencil and one colored pencil?

F 15
G 20
H 30
J 35

13 Every morning the radio station plays 20 songs between noon and 1:00 PM. How many songs does the station play per week in that time slot?

A 70
B 90
C 100
D 140

14 The blue pitcher holds 4 pints of juice. The clear glass pitcher holds 1 pint more than the blue pitcher. How many pints of juice can be made if both pitchers are used?

F 1
G 4
H 5
J 9

GO ON ➡

7 Ⓐ Ⓑ Ⓒ Ⓓ 9 Ⓐ Ⓑ Ⓒ Ⓓ 11 Ⓐ Ⓑ Ⓒ Ⓓ 13 Ⓐ Ⓑ Ⓒ Ⓓ
8 Ⓕ Ⓖ Ⓗ Ⓙ 10 Ⓕ Ⓖ Ⓗ Ⓙ 12 Ⓕ Ⓖ Ⓗ Ⓙ 14 Ⓕ Ⓖ Ⓗ Ⓙ

Answers: 7 C; 8 H; 9 D; 10 J; 11 B; 12 J; 13 D; 14 J

Main Street Skates and Blades

Hourly Rental Fees	Adult	Child	
In-line Skates	$5.00	$3.50	*Weekends*
			Minimum Rental Time: 2 hours
Ice-Skates			
Hockey Skates	5.00	4.00	*Weekday Special*
Figure Skates	3.50	3.00	
			Free adult skate rental with two children's rentals.
Protection Package for In-line Skaters (helmet, knee and elbow pads, wrist guards)	2.50	1.50	

For questions 15–20, use the information in the box above.

15 Jacqui, a fifth grader, rented a pair of in-line skates for 1 hour after school. She had her own helmet and protective gear. How much did Jacqui pay to rent the skates?
A $3.50
B $5.00
C $7.00
D $10.00

16 Marian, an adult, rented in-line skates and the protection package on Saturday. She returned them 50 minutes after she rented them. How much did Marian have to pay?
F $5.00
G $7.50
H $15.00
J $50.00

17 On Saturday Jamal rented a pair of in-line skates to play roller hockey. He rented them at 9:00 AM and returned them at noon. How much did Jamal pay to rent the skates?
A $7.50
B $10.50
C $12.00
D $15.00

18 Mim's family celebrated Mim's tenth birthday with an ice-skating party. Mim's family rented figure skates for 10 children, including Mim. The party lasted for 3 hours. How much did Mim's family pay to rent the skates?
F $30.00
G $90.00
H $105.00
J $120.00

19 On Tuesday Frank rented a pair of child's figure skates. He returned the skates four hours later. How much change did Frank receive from a $20 bill?
A $0.00
B $4.00
C $8.00
D $12.00

20 Joe and his 2 children rented figure skates for 2 hours on Thursday afternoon. How much did Joe pay to rent the three pairs of skates?
F $6.00
G $8.00
H $12.00
J $19.00

15 Ⓐ Ⓑ Ⓒ Ⓓ   17 Ⓐ Ⓑ Ⓒ Ⓓ   19 Ⓐ Ⓑ Ⓒ Ⓓ
16 Ⓕ Ⓖ Ⓗ Ⓙ   18 Ⓕ Ⓖ Ⓗ Ⓙ   20 Ⓕ Ⓖ Ⓗ Ⓙ

Answers: 15 A; 16 H; 17 B; 18 G; 19 C; 20 H

For numbers 21–30, darken the circle for the correct answer to each question.

This bar graph shows the kinds of CD's and audiotapes borrowed from the public library in one month. Study the graph. Then answer questions 21–24.

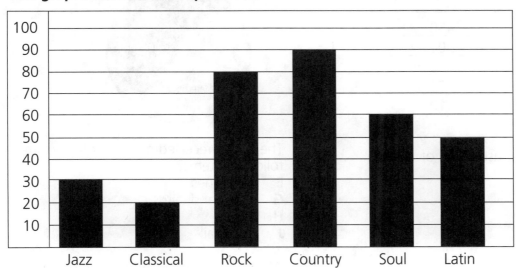

21 Which are the two <u>most</u> popular kinds of music borrowed from the library?
  A soul and Latin
  B jazz and country
  C classical and country
  D rock and country

22 Which two kinds of music are borrowed <u>least often</u> from the library?
  F soul and Latin
  G jazz and classical
  H classical and Latin
  J jazz and soul

23 If borrowers switched from soul to jazz, how many borrowers would then be listening to jazz?
  A 30
  B 50
  C 90
  D 120

24 Which of the following questions <u>cannot</u> be answered using the information on the graph?
  F Is country music more popular than rock?
  G Is classical music more popular than Latin music?
  H How many people borrowed both classical and rock recordings?
  J How much more popular is soul music than jazz?

GO ON

21 Ⓐ Ⓑ Ⓒ Ⓓ   23 Ⓐ Ⓑ Ⓒ Ⓓ
22 Ⓕ Ⓖ Ⓗ Ⓙ   24 Ⓕ Ⓖ Ⓗ Ⓙ

This table shows how homes in one town are heated during the winter. Study the table. Then answer questions 25–27.

Type of Heating	Number of Homes
Oil	450
Gas	300
Coal	50
Wood	75
Solar power	10

25 Which is the <u>least</u> used type of heating in town?
  A gas
  B coal
  C wood
  D solar power

26 Which are the two most popular types of heating?
  F oil and coal
  G oil and gas
  H gas and wood
  J wood and solar power

27 Which of the following is <u>true</u> about gas heat?
  A It is more popular than all other types of heating combined.
  B It is more popular than oil heat.
  C It is the third most popular type of heating.
  D It is more popular than heating by wood or coal.

This pie chart shows what one family received by mail in a month. Study the pie chart. Then answer questions 28–30.

28 The family received most of which of the following items?
  F magazines
  G letters and cards
  H bills
  J junk mail

29 Which of the following items did the family receive the least?
  A magazines
  B letters and cards
  C bills
  D junk mail

30 Which of the following is true about the family's mail?
  F The family receives more magazines than bills.
  G The family receives more junk mail than all other kinds of mail combined.
  H The family receives more cards and letters than magazines.
  J The family receives more bills than junk mail.

25 Ⓐ Ⓑ Ⓒ Ⓓ   27 Ⓐ Ⓑ Ⓒ Ⓓ   29 Ⓐ Ⓑ Ⓒ Ⓓ
26 Ⓕ Ⓖ Ⓗ Ⓙ   28 Ⓕ Ⓖ Ⓗ Ⓙ   30 Ⓕ Ⓖ Ⓗ Ⓙ

Answers: 25 D; **26** G; **27** D; **28** J; **29** C; **30** F

For numbers 31–42, darken the circle for the correct answer to each question.

31 What is the perimeter of the figure below?
  A 20
  B 21
  C 40
  D 42

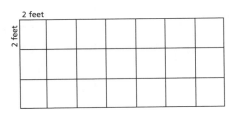

32 Mandy was sent to the store to buy a quart of orange juice. How many 1 pint containers should Mandy buy so that she brings home 1 quart of juice?
  F 2
  G 4
  H 6
  J 8

33 How many squares of paper of the size shown here are needed to completely cover the window?
  A 12
  B 15
  C 18
  D 21

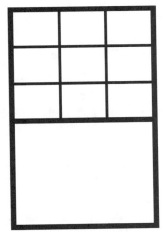

34 What is the length of the ruler from A to B?

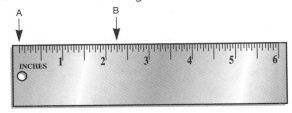

  F 2 inches
  G 2⅛ inches
  H 2¼ inches
  J 2½ inches

35 An object that weighs 2 pounds is placed on one side of a scale. Which of the following weights must be placed on the other side of the scale to make the scale balance?
  A one 1-pound weight and one 8-ounce weight
  B two 8-ounce weights
  C one 1-pound weight and two 8-ounce weights
  D three 8-ounce weights

36 Which temperature would the thermometer show if the temperature rose 10 degrees?
  F 85 degrees
  G 87 degrees
  H 92 degrees
  J 95 degrees

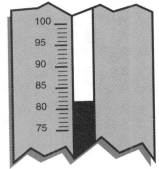

Degrees Fahrenheit

GO ON

31 Ⓐ Ⓑ Ⓒ Ⓓ   33 Ⓐ Ⓑ Ⓒ Ⓓ   35 Ⓐ Ⓑ Ⓒ Ⓓ
32 Ⓕ Ⓖ Ⓗ Ⓙ   34 Ⓕ Ⓖ Ⓗ Ⓙ   36 Ⓕ Ⓖ Ⓗ Ⓙ

Answers: 31 C; **32** F; **33** C; **34** H; **35** C; **36** H

37 What is the area of the rectangle shown?
(Area = length x width)

4 feet

5 feet

A 9 square feet
B 16 square feet
C 20 square feet
D 25 square feet

38 Which of the following figures is a cone?

F

G

H

J

39 The gym teacher sent Jason to get two dozen tennis balls for gym class. Which number below indicates the number of tennis balls Jason had to get?

A 6
B 12
C 24
D 48

40 Which clock face indicates that the time is 6½ hours after 10:00 AM?

F

G

H

J

41 Water freezes at 32 degrees Fahrenheit. How many degrees will the temperature have to rise until it reaches 32 degrees?

A 6 degrees
B 8 degrees
C 10 degrees
D 12 degrees

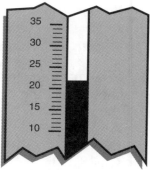

Degrees Fahrenheit

42 What is the length of the ruler from A to B?

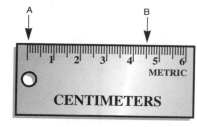

F 4 centimeters
G 4½ centimeters
H 45 centimeters
J 4½ millimeters

GO ON

37 Ⓐ Ⓑ Ⓒ Ⓓ   39 Ⓐ Ⓑ Ⓒ Ⓓ   41 Ⓐ Ⓑ Ⓒ Ⓓ
38 Ⓕ Ⓖ Ⓗ Ⓙ   40 Ⓕ Ⓖ Ⓗ Ⓙ   42 Ⓕ Ⓖ Ⓗ Ⓙ

Answers: 37 C; 38 H; 39 C; 40 J; 41 C; 42 G

For numbers 43–48, darken the circle for the correct answer to each question.

43 The bag of apples contained 9 apples. Kim, Seth, and Tom each ate 1 apple. Which fraction expresses how many of the apples were eaten?

A $\frac{1}{9}$
B $\frac{1}{3}$
C $\frac{2}{3}$
D $\frac{5}{9}$

44 Which of these boxes has $\frac{3}{4}$ of the circles darkened?

F
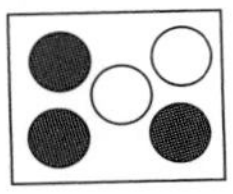

H
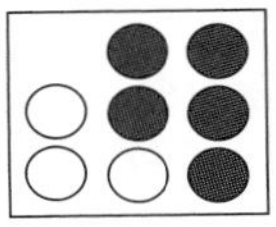

G
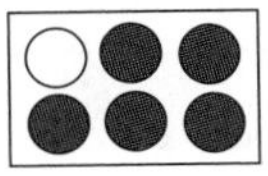

J
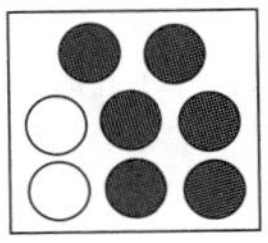

45 Jessica wants to buy a dozen bananas as a snack for her friends. The price marked on the bag of bananas is $2.35. What change will she get from the $5 bill she hands the clerk?

A 1 dollar bill, 4 quarters, 1 dime
B 2 dollar bills, 2 dimes, 2 nickels
C 2 dollar bills, 1 quarter, 5 dimes
D 2 dollar bills, 2 quarters, 3 nickels

46 Rollin wants to buy his brother a pair of gloves for his birthday. The gloves cost $4.95. Rollin has 3 dollar bills and 2 quarters in his pocket. How much more money does Rollin need?

F $1.45
G $1.55
H $1.65
J $1.75

47 Which of the following is equal to $5.25?

A 4 dollar bills, 3 quarters, 8 nickels
B 4 dollar bills, 4 quarters, 6 nickels
C 4 dollar bills, 5 quarters
D 5 dollar bills, 2 dimes, 2 nickels

48 Which fraction tells how many circles in the group are darkened?

F $\frac{1}{2}$
G $\frac{5}{8}$
H $\frac{7}{8}$
J $\frac{2}{3}$

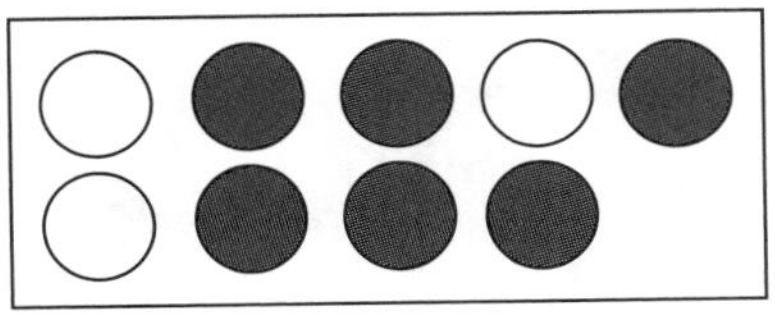

STOP

43 Ⓐ Ⓑ Ⓒ Ⓓ   45 Ⓐ Ⓑ Ⓒ Ⓓ   47 Ⓐ Ⓑ Ⓒ Ⓓ
44 Ⓕ Ⓖ Ⓗ Ⓙ   46 Ⓕ Ⓖ Ⓗ Ⓙ   48 Ⓕ Ⓖ Ⓗ Ⓙ

Answers: 43 B; **44** J; **45** D; **46** F; **47** C; **48** J

Reference and Study Skills

The Reference and Study Skills questions test how well you can find and use information. In this part of *TestWise*, you'll practice all the test-taking strategies and answer-sheet strategies you've been working on since the beginning. You will also learn how to apply these strategies to help you do well on this part of the test.

Learn About the Strategies

Use What You Know

In this part of the test, questions are about many different topics. Thus, you need to read each question carefully. Then think about what you're being asked. Sometimes you'll have data to interpret. This could be a diagram or part of an index. Sometimes you'll be asked questions about where to find information or how to use it.

Use what you know. And know what the test-maker wants. Here's an example. Some questions will ask if you'd look in an encyclopedia, an atlas, or an almanac for certain facts or data. Think about what each kind of book contains. Don't get caught up in quibbles. Yes, an encyclopedia has maps in it. But an atlas is a book of maps—all kinds of maps. If you're asked where to find a map, the answer the test-maker is looking for is probably an atlas.

Read for a Purpose

Look ahead when you begin each page of the Reference and Study Skills test. Notice if some text or diagram is set off in a box. If you see such a box, first read the questions that follow it. The questions will tell you what to do with the boxed material.

Strategy Reminders

Don't forget these important strategies you've been using all along:

Time Strategies	Question Strategies	Answer Sheet Strategies
• Work steadily. Don't stay too long on any one question. • Skip difficult questions. Go back to them later.	• Read the directions care fully. Then put the directions in your own words. Tell yourself what you need to do. • Think of your own answers first. Then check for them in the choices. • Think about the answer choices. Eliminate choices you know right off are wrong.	• As you mark the answer sheet, put your finger on the number of the question you're answering. • Be sure to darken the correct circle. Read the letter inside. • Darken only one answer circle for each question. Darken it completely. • If you change an answer, erase your first answer completely.

28. Using Reference Materials

Directions: Darken the circle for the correct answer to each question.

Sample A

Where would you first look to find a list of Olympic medal winners in speed skating?

A an encyclopedia
B an atlas
C an almanac
D a dictionary

Read the choices. What kind of information do I know each choice contains?

STOP

What does each question want me to do?

1 Which would be the best source of information about polar bears?

A a globe
B a newspaper
C an atlas
D an encyclopedia

2 Where would you first look to find an up-to- date list of the names of the countries in Africa?

F a globe
G an atlas
H an encyclopedia
J an almanac

3 Which would be the best source of information about a person who was just appointed to an important government job?

A a globe
B an almanac
C a newspaper
D an encyclopedia

Use the following information about a book to answer questions 4 and 5.

Bracken Charles.
  Tennis: play like a pro / by Charles Bracken.
  Summary: An introduction to the history and techniques of tennis with advice on how to improve one's game.
    ISBN 0-8167-1932-2 (paperback)
  1. Tennis—Juvenile literature. [1. Tennis].
      I.Title. II. Series.
  GV996.5.B37   1990
  796.342

4 What is the book about?

F professional sports
G Charles Bracken's life
H juvenile literature
J how to play tennis

5 Which number will help you find this book on the library shelves?

A 1990
B 796.342
C 1932-2
D 0-8167

GO ON

If I change an answer, I'll erase the old one completely.

A Ⓐ Ⓑ Ⓒ Ⓓ   2 Ⓕ Ⓖ Ⓗ Ⓙ   4 Ⓕ Ⓖ Ⓗ Ⓙ
1 Ⓐ Ⓑ Ⓒ Ⓓ   3 Ⓐ Ⓑ Ⓒ Ⓓ   5 Ⓐ Ⓑ Ⓒ Ⓓ

Answers: A C; 1 D; 2 J; 3 C; 4 J; 5 B

When I see boxed items, I should read the question first.

Use the Table of Contents from a book about Tennis to answer questions 6–8.

Chapter	Title	Page
1	Tennis Is Terrific	7
2	The Story of Tennis	9
3	What You Need to Play Tennis	13
4	How to Score and Play	19
5	Gripping the Racket	27
6	Good Tennis Technique	35
7	Basic Tennis Strokes	39
8	Putting Spin on the Ball	55
9	Tennis Tips	59
10	Practice	63

6 On which pages are you most likely to find information about the history of tennis?
A pages 7–9
B pages 9–12
C pages 35–39
D pages 59–62

7 Where in this book would you look to find out what the tennis score "4–love" means?
F Chapter 1
G Chapter 3
H Chapter 4
J Chapter 5

8 Where in this book are you most likely to find information on ways to improve your game?
A Chapter 2
B Chapter 3
C Chapter 5
D Chapter 9

Use the list of reference sources, or bibliography, below to answer questions 9–11.

Ancona, George. *Riverkeeper*. New York: Macmillan, 1990.
Arnold, Caroline. *Saving the Peregrine Falcon*. Minneapolis: Carolrhoda Books: 1985.
Canby, Thomas Y. *Our Changing Earth*. Washington, D.C.: National Geographic Society, 1994.
Darling, Kathy. *Manatee on Location*. New York: Lothrop, Lee & Shepard, 1991.
Kudlinski, Kathleen V. Rachel Carson: *Pioneer of Ecology*. New York: Puffin Books, 1988.
Patent, Dorothy Hinshaw. *The Whooping Crane: A Comeback Story*. New York: Clarion Books, 1988.

9 Which of the following topics was this bibliography probably used to prepare a report about?
F how airplanes fly
G how to raise cactus
H how wild animals can be saved from extinction
J how to start a recycling program

10 Which book was published by the National Geographic Society?
A *Riverkeeper*
B *Our Changing Earth*
C *Rachel Carson: Pioneer of Ecology*
D *The Whooping Crane: A Comeback Story*

11 Which of these books may have information that is the most out of date?
F *Riverkeeper*
G *Saving the Peregrine Falcon*
H *Our Changing Earth*
J *Manatee on Location*

STOP

6 Ⓐ Ⓑ Ⓒ Ⓓ   8 Ⓐ Ⓑ Ⓒ Ⓓ   10 Ⓐ Ⓑ Ⓒ Ⓓ
7 Ⓕ Ⓖ Ⓗ Ⓙ   9 Ⓕ Ⓖ Ⓗ Ⓙ   11 Ⓕ Ⓖ Ⓗ Ⓙ

Answers: 6 B; 7 H; 8 D; 9 H; 10 B; 11 G

29. Using the Dictionary

Directions: Darken the circle for the correct answer to each question.

Sample A

Which of these words would be found on a dictionary page that has *boot* and *bottle* as guide words?

A bond
B book
C boom
D botany

Guide words tell the first and the last word. Which of the choices is between *boot* and *bottle* in alphabetical order?

I'll read every question carefully.

1 Which of these words would be found on a dictionary page that has *chuck* and *circle* as guide words?

A chromium
B cinch
C citizen
D city

2 The words *confident* and *conjecture* are guide words on a page. Which of these words would you <u>not</u> find on that page?

F confirm
G confuse
H conscious
J congress

3 You are looking for the main entry word *effective*. Which words would be the guide words on the page where you found the word?

A ear—east
B ecology—edge
C eel—egg
D egret—eject

Use the dictionary entry below to answer questions 4–5.

doze (dohz) v. <dozed, doz-ing> *Verb* **1.** to sleep lightly and briefly; nap. **2.** to fall into a light sleep unintentionally (often followed by *off*): to doze off during class. **3.** to be dull or half asleep. **4.** to pass (time) in napping (often followed by *away*): to doze away the morning. *Noun* **5.** a nap.

4 Which of the definitions of *doze* explains how the word is used in the sentence *He took a quick doze before leaving for work?*

F definition 1
G definition 3
H definition 4
J definition 5

5 What does (dohz) tell you about the word?

A the part of speech
B the pronunciation
C spellings of the verb forms
D the word origin

 STOP

I know I can put every answer in the correct spot on the answer sheet if I pay attention.

A (A)(B)(C)(D)   2 (F)(G)(H)(J)   4 (F)(G)(H)(J)
1 (A)(B)(C)(D)   3 (A)(B)(C)(D)   5 (A)(B)(C)(D)

Answers: A D; 1 B; 2 H; 3 C; 4 J; 5 B

Practice the Strategies

30. Interpreting Visual Materials

Directions: Darken the circle for the correct answer to each question.

Sample A

The Venn diagram below shows where certain sports are usually played.

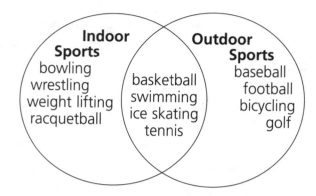

I need to read the questions before I study the diagram.

Which of the following is <u>not</u> usually an indoor sport?
  A bowling
  B wrestling
  C football
  D racquetball

STOP

If I think about my answers, I can get them right.

Use the diagram in Sample A to answer questions 1–4.

1 Which of the following is <u>not</u> usually an outdoor sport?
  A baseball
  B weight lifting
  C bicycling
  D golf

2 What does the center, overlapping part of the Venn diagram show?
  F sports that both men and women play
  G sports played mostly by men
  H sports that can be played indoors or outdoors
  J amateur sports

3 Soccer can be played both indoors and outdoors. Knowing this fact, where in the diagram would you add soccer?
  A to the Indoor Sports part only
  B to the Outdoor Sports part only
  C to both the Indoor Sports part and the Outdoor Sports part
  D to the center, overlapping part only

4 Which of the following sports would usually be classified in the middle part of the diagram?
  F water-skiing
  G parachute jumping
  H mountain climbing
  J in-line skating

STOP

I can't darken two circles next to the same number.

A Ⓐ Ⓑ Ⓒ Ⓓ   2 Ⓕ Ⓖ Ⓗ Ⓙ   4 Ⓕ Ⓖ Ⓗ Ⓙ
1 Ⓐ Ⓑ Ⓒ Ⓓ   3 Ⓐ Ⓑ Ⓒ Ⓓ

Answers: A C; 1 B; 2 H; 3 D; 4 J

88

31. Organizing Information

Directions: Darken the circle for the correct answer to each question.

Sample A

Imagine that you are writing a library report about dolphins. Which information most clearly belongs in the research notes you take for your report?

A library report about dolphins means I'd have to do research. So I'm looking for ideas I could get from books.

- **A** Dolphins are cute.
- **B** Dolphins are air-breathing mammals. They have lungs, not gills.
- **C** Some fish have odd names. A dogfish is a shark. It doesn't look like a dog at all.
- **D** Salmon return to the streams they were born in.

STOP

I'll read the question first. Then I'll read the outline.

Use this part of an outline for a report about dolphins to answer questions 1–4.

Dolphins
I.   Members of the whale family
II. _____
   A. Speed
      1. Can sustain speed of 18 miles per hour
      2. In bursts, can swim 23 to 25 miles per hour
   B. Method of movement
      1. Uses up and down motion of tail, like a whale
      2. Does not use side to side motion of tail, like a fish
   C. Diving ability
      1. Can hold breath for several minutes
      2. _____
   D. _____
      _____

1 Which information best fits on line C.2?
- **A** have layer of blubber under the skin
- **B** has streamlined body
- **C** dives as deep as 1000 feet
- **D** eats mackerel and other fish

2 Which heading best fits on line II?
- **F** How Dolphins reproduce
- **G** Dolphin communication
- **H** Dolphin intelligence
- **J** Characteristics of dolphins

3 Which information best fits under the first heading, Members of the whale family?
- **A** Dolphins are small-toothed whales.
- **B** Dolphins in captivity are not fed live fish.
- **C** Bottlenose dolphins perform in many aquariums.
- **D** Dolphins sometimes get trapped in fish nets.

4 Which could be the most logical choice for heading II.D?
- **F** Legends about dolphins
- **G** Why people like dolphins
- **H** Other physical characteristics
- **J** Dolphins and the fishing industry

STOP

Did I put every answer in the right place? Let me check.

A (A)(B)(C)(D)   2 (F)(G)(H)(J)   4 (F)(G)(H)(J)
1 (A)(B)(C)(D)   3 (A)(B)(C)(D)

Answers: A B; 1 C; 2 J; 3 A; 4 H

Reference and Study Skills

Suggested time: 30 minutes

Read aloud to the class:

The questions on each part of the Reference and Study Skills test are just like the questions you have been practicing.

Read the directions for each group of questions. Read the questions and the answer choices carefully. Then darken the circle for each correct answer. Keep working until you reach the word *STOP* at the bottom of page 94. Then put your pencil down.

For numbers 1–12, darken the circle for the correct answer to each question.

1 Where would you first look to find detailed information about the Vietnam War?
  A an almanac
  B an atlas
  C a dictionary
  D an encyclopedia

2 Where would you first look to find the latitude of Thule in Greenland?
  F a history book
  G a science magazine
  H a globe
  J a dictionary

3 Which would be the best source of information about the career of a baseball player who just retired?
  A a sports magazine
  B an encyclopedia
  C an almanac
  D a nature magazine

4 Which would be the best source of information about a recent scientific discovery?
  F a dictionary
  G an encyclopedia
  H a science magazine
  J an atlas

Use the following information about a book to answer questions 5 and 6.

Stamper, Judith.
    What's it like to be a veterinarian / by Judith Stamper; illustrated by Marcy Dunn Ramsey.
    Summary: Describes the work done by a veterinarian as she treats a variety of small and large animals.
    ISBN 0-8167-1818-0 (paperback)
    1. Veterinarian—Juvenile literature.
    2. Veterinary medicine—Vocational Guidance—Juvenile literature.
[1. Veterinarian. 2. Occupations.]
SF756.S73   1990
636.089

5 What is the title of the book?
  A Stamper Judith
  B Veterinarian—Juvenile literature
  C *What's It Like to Be a Veterinarian*
  D Veterinary medicine—Vocational Guidance

6 When was the book published?
  F 1818
  G 1990
  H 636.089
  J No date is given.

GO ON

1 Ⓐ Ⓑ Ⓒ Ⓓ   3 Ⓐ Ⓑ Ⓒ Ⓓ   5 Ⓐ Ⓑ Ⓒ Ⓓ
2 Ⓕ Ⓖ Ⓗ Ⓙ   4 Ⓕ Ⓖ Ⓗ Ⓙ   6 Ⓕ Ⓖ Ⓗ Ⓙ

Answers: 1 D; 2 H; 3 A; 4 H; 5 C; 6 G

Use the Table of Contents from a book about track and field to answer questions 7–9.

7 In which chapter are you most likely to find information about the best kind of athletic shoes to wear?
A Chapter 1
B Chapter 2
C Chapter 3
D Chapter 4

8 Starting on which pages are you most likely to find information about the javelin throw, the shot put, and other non-running events?
F page 13
G page 25
H page 39
J page 50

9 In which chapter are you most likely to find information about how to get in shape to run track?
A Chapter 2
B Chapter 3
C Chapter 4
D Chapter 5

Use the bibliography, or list of reference sources, below to answer questions 10–12.

Bisel, Sara C. *The Secrets of Vesuvius: Exploring the Mysteries of an Ancient Buried City*. New York: Scholastic, 1990.
Bramwell, Martyn. *Volcanoes and Earthquakes*. New York: Franklin Watts, 1994.
Drury, Roger W. *The Finches' Fabulous Furnace*. New York: Scholastic, 1971.
Gilbreath, Alice Thompson. *Ring of Fire and the Hawaiian Islands and Iceland*. Minneapolis, MN: Dillon Books, 1986.
Krafft, Maurice. *Volcanoes: Fire from the Earth*. New York: H. N. Abrams, 1993.
Setnak, Lewann. *Hawaii Volcanoes*. New York: Crestwood House, 1989.

10 Which of the following topics was this bibliography probably used to prepare a report about?
F Hawaii
G plant life in the tropics
H deserts of the world
J volcanoes

11 Which book is most likely to have information about volcanoes that ring the Pacific Ocean?
A *The Secrets of Vesuvius: Exploring the Mysteries of an Ancient Buried City*
B *Volcanoes and Earthquakes*
C *Ring of Fire and the Hawaiian Islands and Iceland*
D *Volcanoes: Fire from the Earth*

12 Which of the following books is most likely a work of fiction rather than nonfiction?
F *Volcanoes and Earthquakes*
G *The Finches' Fabulous Furnace*
H *Volcanoes: Fire from the Earth*
J *Hawaii Volcanoes*

GO ON ➡

7 Ⓐ Ⓑ Ⓒ Ⓓ   9 Ⓐ Ⓑ Ⓒ Ⓓ   11 Ⓐ Ⓑ Ⓒ Ⓓ
8 Ⓕ Ⓖ Ⓗ Ⓙ   10 Ⓕ Ⓖ Ⓗ Ⓙ   12 Ⓕ Ⓖ Ⓗ Ⓙ

Answers: 7 C; 8 J; 9 D; 10 J; 11 C; 12 G

For numbers 13–20, darken the circle for the correct answer to each question.

13 Which of these words would be found on a dictionary page that has *flexor* and *Florida* as guide words?
  A flat
  B flock
  C florist
  D floss

14 The words *headphone* and *heather* are guide words on a page. Which of these words would you <u>not</u> find on that page?
  F health
  G heat
  H hearty
  J heavy

15 You are looking for the main entry word *hill*. Which words would be the guide words on the page where you found the word?
  A hemp—heritage
  B hermit—hick
  C hide—himself
  D Hindi—hitch

16 Which of these words would be found on a dictionary page that has *jacket* and *janitor* as guide words?
  F jabber
  G jackal
  H jailbird
  J Japan

17 You are looking for the main entry word *cart*. Which words would be the guide words on the page where you found the word?
  A carload—carrot
  B carry—cashew
  C cashier—catapult
  D catch—cause

Use the dictionary entry below to answer questions 18–20.

> **con•vert•i•ble** (kuhn vûr′ tuh buhl) *Adjective*
> **1.** capable of being converted. **2.** having a folding top, as an automobile. **3.** exchangeable for something of equal value: a convertible currency. **4.** having a seat, often with a mattress beneath it, that folds out for use as a bed: a convertible sofa.
> *Noun* **5.** an automobile with a folding top.
> **6.** a convertible sofa. **7.** a convertible bond or security.

18 What does Adjective tell you about the word?
  F its part of speech
  G its pronunciation
  H its syllabication
  J its word origin

19 Which of the definitions of convertible gives the most likely meaning of the word as it is used in the sentence Adam fell asleep on the convertible?
  A definition 1
  B definition 5
  C definition 6
  D definition 7

20 In which of these sentences is definition 1 of the word used correctly?
  F The speedy red convertible roared down the street.
  G Many sports cars are convertibles.
  H Part off the attic is convertible into living space.
  J A convertible sofa can save a great deal of space in a small home.

13 Ⓐ Ⓑ Ⓒ Ⓓ   15 Ⓐ Ⓑ Ⓒ Ⓓ   17 Ⓐ Ⓑ Ⓒ Ⓓ   19 Ⓐ Ⓑ Ⓒ Ⓓ
14 Ⓕ Ⓖ Ⓗ Ⓙ   16 Ⓕ Ⓖ Ⓗ Ⓙ   18 Ⓕ Ⓖ Ⓗ Ⓙ   20 Ⓕ Ⓖ Ⓗ Ⓙ

For numbers 21–24, use the Venn diagram below to answer the questions. Darken the circle for the correct answer to each question.

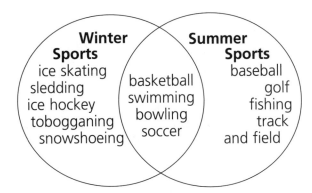

Winter Sports
ice skating
sledding
ice hockey
tobogganing
snowshoeing

basketball
swimming
bowling
soccer

Summer Sports
baseball
golf
fishing
track
and field

---

21 What does the Venn diagram show?
  A when certain sports are usually played
  B who usually plays certain sports
  C why certain sports are popular
  D where certain sports are usually played

22 What would be an accurate title for the overlapping center part of the diagram?
  F West coast sports
  G women's sports
  H sports for the athletically unfit
  J all season sports

23 Where in this diagram would you place skiing?
  A in the Winter Sports section only
  B in the Summer Sports section only
  C in both the Winter Sports and the Summer Sports sections
  D Skiing does not belong in this diagram.

24 Many sports facilities have indoor tennis courts. These courts allow players to enjoy the sport all year round. Knowing this fact, where in the Venn diagram would you place tennis?
  F in the Winter Sports section only
  G in the Summer Sports section only
  H in both the Winter Sports and the Summer Sports sections
  J in the overlapping center part of the diagram

GO ON ▶

---

21 Ⓐ Ⓑ Ⓒ Ⓓ   23 Ⓐ Ⓑ Ⓒ Ⓓ
22 Ⓕ Ⓖ Ⓗ Ⓙ   24 Ⓕ Ⓖ Ⓗ Ⓙ

For numbers 25–30, darken the circle for the correct answer to each question.

25 Imagine that you are writing a library report about dogs. Which information most clearly belongs in the research notes you take for your report?
A My dog likes to chase cats.
B Dogs have pretty hair.
C Veterinarians are animal doctors. Being a vet can be rewarding.
D Dependability is one reason a dog is selected as a guide dog for the blind.

Use this part of an outline for a report about dogs to answer questions 26–30.

Dogs
I. Working dogs
  A. Police dogs
    1. Bloodhounds
    2. Search and rescue dogs
    3. _____
  B. Herding dogs
  C. Hunting dogs
II. Helping dogs
  A. Guide dogs for the blind
    1. German shepherds
    2. Labrador retrievers
  B. _____
III. Show dogs
  A. Circus dogs
  B. Movie and TV dogs
    1. _____
      _____
    2. _____
      _____

26 Which category of information best fits on line II.B?
F Racing dogs
G Mutts
H Assistance dogs for the hearing impaired
J The ancestors of modern dogs

27 You want to include information about Siberian Huskies and other sled dogs. Which is the most likely category to put this information in.
A Working dogs
B Helping dogs
C Show dogs
D Guide dogs for the blind

28 Which kind of dog are you most likely to include on line I.A.3?
F dogs such as dachshunds that were once used as hunting dogs but are now mostly kept as pets
G dogs such as greyhounds that are swift racing dogs
H dogs trained to catch Frisbees in the park
J dogs trained to sniff out bombs or illegal drugs

29 Which dog are you most likely to include in your outline on line III.B.1?
A a dog trained to find lost hikers and skiers
B a dog trained as a police dog
C a dog in a movie fellow students would recognize
D a dog trained to herd sheep

30 You want to include information about keeping dogs healthy. Which is the most likely place in the outline for this information?
F Add it under I.A.
G Add it in place of I.B.
H Add it under II.
J Add it in a new category of its own.

STOP

25 Ⓐ Ⓑ Ⓒ Ⓓ   27 Ⓐ Ⓑ Ⓒ Ⓓ   29 Ⓐ Ⓑ Ⓒ Ⓓ
26 Ⓕ Ⓖ Ⓗ Ⓙ   28 Ⓕ Ⓖ Ⓗ Ⓙ   30 Ⓕ Ⓖ Ⓗ Ⓙ

Answers: 25 D; 26 H; 27 A; 28 J; 29 C; 30 J

Supplementary Answer Key to the Timed Practice Tests

Your students may record their answers to the Timed Practice Tests either at the bottom of each test page or on copies of the separate answer sheet printed on pages 9 and 10.

If your students use the separate answer sheet, below is the answer key for the Timed Practice Tests.

TEST 1. Vocabulary (*pages 17–21*)

1 B; **2** H; **3** C; **4** F; **5** D; **6** F; **7** D; **8** H; **9** B; **10** H; **11** B; **12** J; **13** D; **14** H; **15** B; **16** J; **17** B; **18** F; **19** C; **20** G; **21** C; **22** F; **23** A; **24** H; **25** C; **26** G; **27** D; **28** B; **29** H; **30** B; **31** H; **32** A; **33** H; **34** B; **35** G; **36** B; **37** J; **38** D; **39** F; **40** C; **41** H; **42** A; **43** G; **44** D; **45** G; **46** B; **47** H; **48** A; **49** H; **50** B; **51** J; **52** A; **53** H

TEST 2. Reading Comprehension (*pages 28–32*)

1 B; **2** F; **3** B; **4** G; **5** D; **6** H; **7** B; **8** J; **9** C; **10** F; **11** B; **12** F; **13** D; **14** G; **15** C; **16** F; **17** B; **18** H; **19** C; **20** J; **21** A; **22** H; **23** A; **24** J; **25** B; **26** G; **27** A; **28** F; **29** C; **30** H; **31** A; **32** F; **33** A; **34** H

TEST 3. Spelling (*pages 36–37*)

1 C; **2** F; **3** D; **4** G; **5** C; **6** J; **7** D; **8** G; **9** B; **10** G; **11** A; **12** H; **13** C; **14** F; **15** D; **16** H; **17** C; **18** H; **19** C; **20** H; **21** B; **22** F; **23** A; **24** H

TEST 4. Language Mechanics (*pages 41–42*)

1 A; **2** H; **3** B; **4** H; **5** A; **6** H; **7** D; **8** H; **9** B; **10** G; **11** B; **12** G; **13** A; **14** G; **15** B; **16** H; **17** D; **18** J

TEST 5. Language Expression (*pages 51–57*)

1 C; **2** F; **3** C; **4** J; **5** B; **6** J; **7** C; **8** H; **9** B; **10** J; **11** B; **12** H; **13** A; **14** J; **15** C; **16** G; **17** B; **18** H; **19** B; **20** H; **21** D; **22** G; **23** A; **24** H; **25** D; **26** G; **27** B; **28** J; **29** C; **30** G; **31** D; **32** F; **33** B; **34** G; **35** C; **36** J; **37** C; **38** J; **39** D; **40** H

TEST 6. Math Computation (*pages 63–66*)

1 D; **2** F; **3** D; **4** K; **5** C; **6** G; **7** D; **8** F; **9** D; **10** H; **11** B; **12** J; **13** D; **14** G; **15** A **16** G; **17** A; **18** F; **19** C; **20** F; **21** C; **22** F; **23** B; **24** H; **25** A; *26* J; **27** E; **28** H; **29** B; **30** J; **31** A; **32** J; **33** C; **34** K; **35** D; **36** F; **37** C; **38** G

TEST 7. Math Concepts and Applications (*pages 76–83*)

1 C; 2 J; **3** A; **4** H; **5** D; **6** F; **7** C; **8** H; **9** D; **10** J; **11** B; **12** J; **13** D; **14** J; **15** A; **16** H; **17** B; **18** G; **19** C; **20** H; **21** D; **22** G; **23** C; **24** H; **25** D; **26** G; **27** D; **28** J; **29** C; **30** F; **31** C; **32** F; **33** C; **34** H; **35** C; **36** H; **37** C; **38** H; **39** C; **40** J; **41** C; **42** G; **43** B; **44** J; **45** D; **46** F; **47** C; **48** J

TEST 8. Reference and Study Skills (*pages 90–94*)

1 D; **2** H; **3** A; **4** H; **5** C; **6** G; **7** C; **8** J; **9** D; **10** J; **11** C; **12** G; **13** B; **14** J; **15** C; **16** H; **17** B; **18** F; **19** C; **20** H; **21** A; **22** J; **23** A; **24** J; **25** D; **26** H; **27** A; **28** J; **29** C; **30** J

Alternative Assessment Strategies

The computerized reports that test-makers provide to record the results of standardized testing give teachers and schools an extensive portrait of student achievement. But even the most vocal advocates of standardized testing will agree that these reports do not provide a total portrait of what students have accomplished. For this kind of data, teachers nationwide are turning toward alternative forms of assessment. The most widespread of these forms is portfolio assessment.

What Is Portfolio Assessment?

Portfolio assessment documents student achievement over time. First developed to gauge students' growth as writers, portfolio assessment has grown beyond collecting writing samples to encompass written works and other projects developed in all content areas. Portfolios can include artwork, videotapes, audio tapes, science experiments, and other forms of personal and intellectual expression—whatever teacher and student agree should be in the portfolio.

Choice and Who Chooses

The hallmark of portfolio assessment is choice. Early in the year, students and teachers discuss what a portfolio is and how they will go about compiling theirs.

- The teacher and student decide together what should be in the portfolio. Will it be only the student's best work? Will it be finished works only or should it also present works in progress? Should there be a required number of works in the portfolio by year's end, as a goal for students to aim toward, or will contents reflect the pace of each student's learning? These and many other questions specific to a teacher's classroom must be addressed and resolved early in the year.

- Of great importance in a program of portfolio evaluation is who chooses the items that go into the portfolio. Ideally, the choice is the student's. The process helps develop the student's sense of ownership of what he or she is learning. The student become more actively involved in and responsible for learning and for recognizing when his or her work has improved.

- Standards are also important. At the start of the year, teachers and students need to work together to develop criteria for the level of work that will go into a portfolio.
    For written work, teachers may want students to include a "baseline sample" against which students can measure their progress over the course of the year.

Advantages of Portfolio Assessment for the Teacher

Since portfolio assessment encourages ongoing communication about projects and progress, teachers have more opportunities than conventional assessment methods allow to identify a learner's strengths and weaknesses and thereby individualize learning.

The portfolio itself is an excellent means to show parents during teacher conferences how their children are performing in school. Parents see more than a grade. They see growth and progress in a concrete, tangible form. Teachers may also use contents of the portfolio to discuss students' work with administrators, counselors, and other teachers.

Teachers who plan to adopt portfolio assessment as an evaluation tool should communicate with parents their plans for the year and build an understanding of how portfolio assessment works. Parents will see for themselves the benefits it affords their children's education.